IN THE EVENT

D0901596

FLORIDA STATE
UNIVERSITY LIBRARIES

AUG 18 2008

TALLAHASSEE, FLORIDA

MERIDIAN

Crossing Aesthetics

Werner Hamacher

& David E. Wellbery

Editors

Stanford
University
Press

Stanford
California
1999

IN THE EVENT

Reading Journalism, Reading Theory

Deborah Esch

PN
4731
.E66
1999

Stanford University Press
Stanford, California

© 1999 by the Board of Trustees
of the Leland Stanford Junior University

Printed in the United States of America

CIP data appear at the end of the book

For Phil

A gift comes from the past, the residue of what we have already done. The unwanted part. Then one day there is revealed to us another potential which we are now ready for. To find from our own past the needed confidence: out of violence comes a calm.

—Isamu Noguchi, *The Isamu Noguchi Garden Museum*

Acknowledgments

This book owes its existence to the encouragement and example of Stephen Andrews, Ian Balfour, Colin Campbell, Nancy Campbell, Cathy Caruth, Cynthia Chase, Ann Diego, Susan Ehrlich, Lois Esch, David Esch, John Greyson, Werner Hamacher, Phil Jackson, Tom Keenan, Tom Levin, Tres Pyle, Andrew Ross, John Santos, Alan Story, Kendall Thomas, Sam Weber, and Alexander Wilson. I am grateful to Giovanna Scarpa for her part in making possible the final stages of research and writing; to Helen Tartar for her patience and generosity; to Kate Warne and Karen Hellekson for their editorial expertise; and to the crew at Bar Italia for dependable espresso and shelter from the storm.

Earlier versions of several of the chapters have appeared as follows (all have been revised since their prior publication):

"The invasion of the corpus snatchers" first appeared as the chapter entitled "Deconstruction" in *Redrawing the Boundaries: The Transformation of English and American Literary Studies*, edited by Stephen Greenblatt and Giles Gunn (New York: Modern Language Association of America, 1992), 374–91.

"The work to come" first appeared in *diacritics* 20, no. 3 (fall 1990): 28–49.

"No time like the present" first appeared in *Culture Lab*, edited by Brian Boigon (New York: Princeton Architectural Press, 1993), 61–78.

"Missing in action" first appeared in *Alphabet City* 1, no. 1 (summer 1991): 19–21.

"The test of time" first appeared in French under the title "Le deuil de la télévision," *Surfaces* 1, no. 1 (fall 1991): 1–14.

"Only a question of time, etc." first appeared under the title "Alice James and the Right to Death," *Public* 9 (1994): 131–49.

Thanks to the original copyright holders (Modern Language Association, Johns Hopkins University Press, Princeton Architectural Press) for permission to reprint.

Contents

Illustrations

Sarah Charlesworth, "*Herald Tribune*: January 19–20, 1991." Detail from "*Herald Tribune*: January 18–February 28, 1991." Thirty-six black-and-white photographic prints. Collection of the artist, courtesy Jay Gorney Modern Art, New York.

Introduction

The impulse to gather the following essays in a single volume came initially as part of my response to a contemporary work that exemplifies the burden of reading imposed by the correlation of the textual and the historical, the order of language and the order of events. Under the general title *Modern History*, American artist Sarah Charlesworth has since 1977 created a remarkable series that makes available for analysis the visual syntax of what we call "the news" as reported in a range of publications. An early component of the series, "*Herald Tribune*: November 1977," reproduces in sequence the front pages of the *International Herald Tribune* (the self-styled "global newspaper") for a period of one month in the form of photocopies of the "originals" that maintain their scale and layout but excise the written text, preserving only a constellation of images whose referential efficacy depends on the viewer's inevitably fallible memory. Fourteen years later, the artist provided a counterpoint to this examination of the day-to-day presentation of the news with another subseries that duplicates in the same manner the *Tribune*'s front-page coverage of a more readily identifiable event or set of events: the war in the Persian Gulf (a focus of Part II, below) from January 18 to February 28, 1991. As one curator has observed, "While the format of the two works is identical, the specific time frame of the 1991 work indicates a shift in emphasis from the daily unfolding of general events that comprise 'the news,' as in the

1977 piece, to the actual visual presentation of war. What emerges beneath the apparent display of power is a striking view of that which is not said, not shown, not known" (Grachos, "Contemporary Currents," n.p.).

Striking indeed is *Modern History*'s visual elaboration of several of the theoretical claims that traverse the readings that follow, claims about the resistance of historical events to perception, to cognition, and to language. In Charlesworth's own assessment, the series affords its viewers "the experience of a codified relation to an absent event . . . through the media context, through the ordering of its surface . . . the experience of being acted upon, being called upon . . . to participate . . . in the rhetorical manifestations of power" ("Unwriting," n.p.). The multiple mediations involved in the ordering of *Modern History* insist that its reduplicated photographs are not mimetic representations of events but rather allegorical signs alluding to an anteriority that cannot be recovered as presence or recuperated as certain knowledge or recollection.

Inscribed in these appropriated images is a tacit argument about photography as a medium of historiography, which I can only begin to translate in the brief scope of an introduction to other work. Charlesworth's redeployed front pages demonstrate, by and for example, that the punctual unity (the "then and there") that seems to define the photographic image is an idealized fiction. Often the illusion of instantaneity is motivated by a vested interest in erasing from the image the multiple, heterogeneous times that went into its production, positioning, and eventual reception. But these constitutive distances, or differences, cannot be *represented* in the photograph; rather, the passing of time, and the time of its own passing (as image of the past) can only be *figured* there. Thus we are called upon to search the image for precisely what it occults: the differential times that characterize the medium's structure and effects.

This is the responsibility to which we are summoned in no uncertain terms in Walter Benjamin's writings on the function of the image, and specifically the photographic image, for historiography. In the well-known formulation in the "Theses on the Concept of History," for example, Benjamin claims that "The true image of the past flits by. The past can be seized only as an image which flashes up at the instant when it can be recognized and is never seen again. . . . For every image of the past that is not recognized by the present as one of its own concerns threatens to disappear irretrievably" (225). In these terms, the possibility of reading and writing history is tied to the endurance of traces of the past, and their coming to legibility—allegorically—at a given time. For Benjamin, this critical point is a moment of danger, when historical meaning is itself at risk. Historiography confronts this menace, testing its mettle in the attempt to grasp fleeting images. Viewed in this light, Charlesworth's series makes explicit what the image of the past always gives us to read: the threat of its own passing, its degradation and eventual disappearance. Thus the photographic image takes place in the mode of a pledge: Everything may be preserved for history. But if what is preserved is in the process of disappearing, perhaps what is kept is only the promise.

If in *Modern History* it is allegory that "codifies" our relation to history (understood in the concrete terms of the material specificity of the event), we find ourselves in a realm mapped most rigorously in recent literary studies. In particular, the theoretical writings of Paul de Man (which I address in Part I) elaborate through a range of exemplary readings the ways in which allegory's constitutive temporal dimension, the difference that divides the allegorical sign from its referent, disrupts our ready presumptions of continuity and simultaneity between the image and what we take it to represent. Those presumptions, as he argues in his pivotal essay "The Rhetoric of Temporality," in turn ground an understanding of the relation of subject to object "in which the experience of the object takes on the form of a perception or a sensation. The ultimate intent of the image is synthesis," and "the mode of the synthesis is defined as symbolic by the priority conferred on the initial moment of sensory perception"—that is, on the aesthetic moment (193). The consequences of de Man's analysis are far-reaching indeed, for the symbol as traditionally defined proves to be the linguistic condition of possibility of a certain claim for the power and autonomy of the aesthetic. I would argue that a text such as *Modern History* lays bare the ideological character of a claim that may only pretend to the status of theory.

In Charlesworth's visual allegory, the unmistakable wearing away of the "original" in the process of photoduplication and the deliberate masking or excision of the written text also figure the process of biodegradation that Jacques Derrida has posited as the eventual fate of things cultural as well as natural. Derrida's inquiry into the translatability to culture of the figure of the "biodegradable" takes place in the context of his response to the emergence of de Man's wartime journalism and its impact on readers—and nonreaders—of the latter's theoretical work (treated at length in Part I, Chapter 2, below). That response, offered in the two-part form of his essay "Like the Sound of the Sea Deep Within a Shell: Paul de Man's War" and a subsequent series of diary fragments collected under the title "Biodegradables," was "set in motion by this question: What remains? What is '*survivre*' (living on, surviving, *Fortleben*, *Überleben*)? How did these newspaper articles and everything they record resist time? From what distance and by means of what detours?" ("Biodegradables," 863–64). Derrida's account redirects us to de Man's early review of Henri de Montherlant's *Solstice de juin*, published in the Belgian daily *Le Soir* in 1941, and the young journalist's strategic citation of the text under consideration:

> By quoting de Man quoting what is, in sum, Montherlant's wager ("'"To the writers who have given too much to current affairs for the past few months, I predict, for that part of their work, the most complete oblivion. When I open the newspapers and journals of today, I hear the indifference of the future rolling over them, just as one hears the sound of the sea when one holds certain seashells up to the ear"'"), I called attention to the paradoxical and cruel survival of an error or a lost wager. ("Biodegradables," 864)

What engaged Derrida in this journalistic exercise

> was the transmission at a distance, the teleprogrammatrix, the delays, detours, halts, the play of mediation, of the media, and of the immediacy in the storing and routing of a still readable or audible archive. . . . What interested me above all was the *structure of this event* in the enor-

> mous mass of that which it conditions or in which it participates: first an error of appraisal (Montherlant's then de Man's quoting Montherlant on the subject of the disappearance of the newspapers and the indifferent amnesia that awaits them). The error sees itself cruelly belied by history, which takes charge of its own survival, the archival survival of this very error, of this utterance and of this quotation. . . . In a newspaper, someone quotes an error while making in his turn an error on the subject of the nonsurvival of newspapers and assures *in that very way, in determined conditions*, the survival of the newspaper article, of the quotation, and of the requotation of these very errors. As such! It is as if I were assuring the survival of a text by mistakenly saying of it: "I bet this will not survive." ("Biodegradables," 864–65)

As its epigraph suggests, the present volume's trajectory of reading is likewise guided by the question of what, over time, will remain, and in what form. More specifically, given the differential rhetorical and temporal conditions of journalism, including the form of the journal or diary as well as newspaper articles and televised broadcasts, what is the nature of its legacy to cultural memory or amnesia? The question, if not its definitive answer, is figured in Charlesworth's canny quotation of already degraded photographs and her deliberate deletion of the written reports that accompanied them.

In effect, these essays place their own wager on the validity of the broader lesson that Derrida draws from his encounter with de Man's work, early and late:

> One of the most necessary gestures of a deconstructive understanding of history consists . . . in transforming things by exhibiting writings, genres, textual strata (which is also to say . . . exhibiting institutional, economic, political, pulsive [and so on] "realities") that have been repulsed, repressed, devalorized, minoritized, delegitimated, occulted by hegemonic canons, in short, all that which certain forces have attempted to melt down into the anonymous mass of an unrecognizable culture, to "(bio)degrade" in the common compost of a memory said to be living and organic. From this point of view, deconstructive interpretation and writing would come along, without any soteriological mission, to 'save,' in some sense, lost heritages. This is not done without a certain counterevaluation, in particular a political one. One

does not exhume just anything. And one transforms while exhuming. ("Biodegradables," 821)

Impelled by such a necessity, *In the Event* assembles readings of evanescent texts and textual configurations, including newspaper reports and "live" broadcasts, as well as a pair of journals of the kind conventionally relegated to marginal status, devalorized on the basis of their genre or mode as well as their noncanonical authorship (Part III, below). For better or worse, the book's argument relies to a great extent on the force of the examples enlisted to make it: a force that is irreducible to their semantic content and hence itself resistant to degradation, which is to say, to time.

Finally, the chapters collected here place particular emphasis on the ideology of realism that underpins the related modes of newspaper article, "live" broadcast, and journal. If the "reality" to which this realism lays claim is "not simply a *factum* but could also be an ideological construct, a fiction or *fictum*" (as Werner Hamacher writes in the context of his own response to de Man's wartime journalism in "Journals, Politics" [454]), then these readings must also seek to gauge the pertinence and adequacy of any theoretical framework brought to bear in the analysis of the determinants and functions of the realism upon which the journalist as well as the diarist rely. At a minimum, theory serves to mediate the immediacy (the realm of "actual experience") to which the realist appeals: to elicit the ways in which what we take to be historical events are produced, even constituted, by an array of discursive technologies "in which language and history, reduced to the status of 'news,' not only serve as commodities but as 'proof of reality' for whatever and whoever is involved in the general movement of its utterances" (Hamacher, "Journals, Politics," 464). The investigation of the technical production of "reality" yields crucial consequences for thinking history as of the order of an event that leaves a material (and hence to some extent legible) trace on the world. Whether that trace takes the form of a faded photograph, a ruined mosque, or an enigmatic diary entry, our responsibility to it always casts us in the role of reader, confronting the rhetorical mode and referential authority of the text, whatever its medium.

PART ONE

Journals, theories

§ 1 The invasion of the corpus snatchers

(Some journalistic versions of "theory")

In April 1987, the *Washington Post* ran a front-page story disclosing that American officials had known since 1979 that the Soviet Union was planting listening devices in the U.S. embassy complex under construction in Moscow. According to then–Assistant Secretary of State Robert E. Lamb, a special counterintelligence task force had been set up to find and "neutralize" the devices. "We knew the Soviets were going to bug us," Lamb testified before the House Subcommittee on International Operations. But counterintelligence did not anticipate that the Soviets would use "the structure itself as part of the bugging": The devices, as it turned out, were embedded in the precast concrete blocks and reinforcing bars used in the construction of the embassy walls and floors. Work on the edifice was halted only in August 1985, six years after construction had begun. Richard Dertadian, deputy assistant secretary of the State Department's Foreign Building Office, reported to the committee that the government was contemplating as one of its options the "deconstruction" of the top two or three floors of the embassy chancery. Asked what it might cost to "deconstruct" part of the building, Dertadian ventured that the cost would equal roughly what the U.S. had already spent to erect the chancery, with the total amounting to most of the sum appropriated for construction in the first place (Ottaway, "U.S. Alerted," A1, A17).[1]

A story of superpower intrigue reported prominently, if belatedly (befitting the *Post*)—history chronicled more or less as it unfolds—may also serve as an allegory of events taking place elsewhere, in the ostensibly rarified and circumscribed sphere of literary and cultural studies. The reiteration, in quotation marks, of "deconstruction" and "deconstruct" in the reported exchange appears to be an instance of one institutional jargon citing (however unwittingly) another, translating what has become a more or less technical term in academic discourse into a usage of another order, which is cited in turn by the media.[2] But is it possible in such a case strictly to demarcate, or even denominate, the respective realms: academic, bureaucratic, journalistic? What is at stake in their articulation, especially when it confers priority of place on one over another? And what justifies reading this report of a Cold War skirmish (whose geopolitics are already outdated, a thing of the past, at least as of the "deconstruction" of that boundary of boundaries, the Berlin Wall, and the profound political and social transformations that have since taken place) as an allegory of whatever "deconstruction" may have to do with redrawing the boundaries of, for example, literary and cultural studies in the North American academy?

The seeking and acquiring of intelligence by means of acoustic surveillance has long been a predictable part of the give-and-take of international relations. The value of such knowledge lies, of course, in its translatability into the terms of power vis-à-vis the adversary. Not foreseen in this episode was the transformation, via a certain technology, of the very architecture of the institutional structure into a relay of information potentially damaging to the embassy and to the territorial (or, in the parlance of the planners, the "national security") interests it represents: "U.S. counterintelligence agents had first thought they could 'neutralize' and turn their knowledge of Soviet bugging efforts to the advantage of the United States, but then discovered the devices were planted inside the building materials" (Ottaway, "U.S. Alerted," A1). Despite the "highly sophisticated countermeasures" brought to bear on the situation, officials were thus compelled to acknowledge—well after the fact—the vulnerability of the structure itself to wholesale "deconstruction."[3]

Language, knowledge, power, technology, media, institutions: These are among the persistent preoccupations of deconstruction as it has come to intervene in and transform literary studies, among other disciplines and practices. Moreover, the *Post*'s account employs

> a figure of what some might be tempted to see as the dominant metaphorical register, indeed the allegorical bent of 'deconstruction,' a certain architectural rhetoric. One first locates, in an architectonics, in the art of the system, . . . that which, from the outset, threatens the coherence and the internal order of the construction. . . . It is required by the architecture which it nevertheless, in advance, deconstructs from within. It assures its cohesion while situating in advance . . . the site that lends itself to a deconstruction to come. (Derrida, "Art of Memoires," 72)

A temporal operation thus complicates from the outset the spatial metaphorics of the architectural model (signaled, for example, in the temporal ironies of the embassy incident: the foreknowledge of the Soviet bugging operation, the failure to anticipate its use of "precast" materials, the post hoc disclosure):

> the very condition of a deconstruction may be at work, in the work, *within* the system to be deconstructed; it may *already* be located there, already at work . . . participating in the construction of what it at the same time threatens to deconstruct. One might then be inclined to reach this conclusion: deconstruction is not an operation that supervenes *afterwards*, from the outside, one fine day; it is always already at work in the work. . . . Since the disruptive force of deconstruction is always already contained within the architecture of the work, all one would finally have to do to be able to deconstruct, given this *always already*, is to do memory work. (Derrida, "Art of Memoires," 73)

Yet as Derrida reminds his readers time and again, the multiple logics and rhetorics of deconstruction do not depend upon the figuration strongly suggested by the term's association with the architectonic, with a system of assembly or reassembly; for it is precisely "everything that can be reassembled under the rubric of logocentrism," including many of the foundational concepts of Western metaphysics, that deconstructive analysis subjects to scrutiny. Logocentrism is understood to comprise "the system of speech, consciousness, meaning, presence, truth, etc.," which is itself an effect—an effect to be analyzed—of "a more and more powerful historical unfolding of a general writing," a multiple network of traces that cannot be subsumed under philosophy's traditional understanding of writing as a medium of communication at one remove from the plenitude and self-presence of speech nor exhausted by "a hermeneutic deciphering," by "the decoding of meaning or truth" ("Signature Event Context," 329). In the "very schematic" but still indispensable formulation of a general deconstructive strategy that concludes "Signature Event Context," Derrida notes that "an opposition of metaphysical concepts (for example, speech/writing, presence/absence, etc.) is never the face-to-face of two terms, but a hierarchy and an order of subordination." And he goes on to assert what the *Post* allegory may be said to confirm, that "Deconstruction cannot limit itself or proceed immediately to a neutralization" of such oppositions, nor can it be content to inhabit, however uneasily, the field they constitute; rather, "it must, by means of a double gesture, a double science, a double writing, practice an *overturning* of the classical opposition *and* a general *displacement* of the system. It is only on this condition that deconstruction will provide itself the means with which to *intervene* in the field of oppositions that it criticizes, which is also a field of nondiscursive forces" ("Signature Event Context," 329).

The double gesture of deconstructive intervention, then, is not restricted to or determined by architectural metaphors or the conceptual and nonconceptual orders they may be taken to figure. "It doesn't mean, for example, that we have to destroy something which is built—physically built or culturally built or theoretically built," for deconstruction puts in question the authority of precisely these rhetorical structures: "the metaphor of foundations, of superstructures, what Kant calls 'architectonic' etc., as well as the concept of the *arche*" (Derrida, "In Discussion," 8). Yet the recent appropriation and elaboration of deconstructive thought in architectural theory and practice is one indication that this "dominant metaphorical register," if not necessary or inevitable, is at any rate telling, not least (as the *Post* allegory once again attests) in the reminder it affords of the way in which deconstruction may be bound to and implicated in structures already in place, as well as susceptible to its own analysis: "Operating necessarily from the inside, borrowing all the strategic and economic resources of subversion from the old structure, borrowing them structurally, that is to say without being able to isolate their elements and atoms, the enterprise of deconstruction always in a certain way falls prey to its own work" (Spivak, Translator's Introduction, 24).

Such considerations must figure in any attempt to assess the cumulative effects of deconstruction on scholarship, criticism, and pedagogy and to redress misunderstandings and misrepresentations of those effects. The most recurrent of the latter have characterized deconstruction as "pure verbalism, as a denial of the reality principle in the name of absolute fictions" (de Man, "Resistance to Theory," 10), as a reduction to linguistic phenomena of nondiscursive forces, including those presumed to constitute the social and historical contexts of literary production and reception, characterizations that seem to forget or ignore deconstruction's beginnings as a critique of logocentrism. To some extent, this misunderstanding and its perpetuation (along with the concomitant charges of political quietism or conservatism) are themselves effects of certain features of deconstruction's initial intervention into the field or fields of literary and cultural studies, particularly in North America. The keen interest in Saussurean linguistics, Lacanian psychoanalysis, and structuralist anthropology that marked the theoretical scene in France in the 1960s and 1970s was a determining consideration for deconstructive analysis, whose evolving concerns and strategies have been highly responsive to time and place. And given the specificity of its beginnings in a critical engagement with the tradition of Western philosophy (e.g., the critique of speculative dialectics—its determination of difference as contradiction and its resolution of classical binary oppositions through an idealizing, totalizing third term—by way of a Derridean "logic" of *différance*), deconstruction did not at the outset always concern itself explicitly with a thematics of politics or history. But a reflection on the political dimensions of deconstructive analysis and of the fields in which it intervenes was and is readable, for example, in Derrida's early and repeated insistence on the necessity, in reading philosophical as well as literary texts, of overturning and displacing the terms of their foundational structures:

> To do justice to this necessity is to recognize that in a classical philosophical opposition we are not dealing with the peaceful coexistence of a *vis-à-vis*, but rather with a violent hierarchy. One of the two terms governs the other (axiologically, logically, etc.), or has the upper hand. To deconstruct the opposition, first of all, is to overturn the hierarchy at a given moment. To overlook this phase of overturning is to forget the conflictual and subordinating structure of opposition. Therefore one might proceed too quickly to a *neutralization* that *in practice* would leave the previous field untouched, leaving one no hold on the previous opposition, thereby preventing any means of *intervening* in the field effectively. We know what always have been the *practical* (particularly *political*) effects of *immediately* jumping *beyond* oppositions, and of protests in the simple form of *neither* this *nor* that. (*Positions*, 41)

And if deconstruction did not consistently foreground from the first its own potential as an instrument and a mode of institutional critique, the indissociability of deconstructive textual analysis from questions of disciplinarity and the institution, of "an *institutionalized system of interpretation* in which precisely the question of the institution itself had come to be obliterated," has become increasingly evident over the course of its elaborations (Weber, Introduction, ix). Deconstruction and its corresponding pedagogy, often in productive conjunction with feminism and psychoanalysis, have challenged and dislocated disciplinary boundaries, including those associated with literature and philosophy as well as history, anthropology, theology, and law. More fundamentally still, Derrida's investigations of the institutional and political conditions of academic work include studies of the history of the university (and its founding "principle of reason") and its roles and responsibilities with regard to the politics of research and teaching in advanced technological societies. At stake in these analyses is the implication, as well as the transformative potential, of what appear to be the least end-oriented and programmable of disciplines (including literature) in larger military-industrial, technoeconomic networks.

Samuel Weber has formulated succinctly the emerging emphasis on the institutional and political in the trajectory of Derrida's work of reading and writing:

> Whereas the earlier, more classically deconstructive writings of Derrida—up to *Dissemination*, which can be seen as a kind of pivot—sought to demonstrate the problematic status of certain major attempts, in the Western intellectual tradition, at systematic closure, i.e., at institutionalization, his subsequent writings have carried this demonstration further and, in a certain sense, in a different direction. Having established a certain structural instability in the most powerful attempts to provide modes of structuration, it was probably inevitable that Derrida should then begin to explore the other side of the coin, the fact that, *undecidability notwithstanding*, decisions are *in fact* taken, power *in fact* exercised, traces *in fact* instituted. It is the highly ambivalent *making* of such *facts* that has increasingly imposed itself upon and throughout the more recent writings of Derrida as well as upon the field of problems and practices associated with his work. (Weber, Introduction, x)

Weber's own work, together with that of Wlad Godzich, Werner Hamacher, Thomas Keenan, Philippe Lacoue-Labarthe, Avital Ronell, Cathy Caruth, Gayatri Spivak, and many others, attests to the multiple ways in which deconstructive analysis can be brought effectively to bear on a range of institutional and political questions as they inform literary and cultural studies.

Derrida himself has insisted on the necessity of engaging texts not simply or primarily on the basis of their discursive contents, "but always as institutional structures, and, as is commonly said, as being political-juridical-sociohistorical—none of these last words being reliable enough to be used easily" ("Some Statements and Truisms," 86). In an interview whose express focus is deconstruction and architecture, he contests yet again the charges of verbalism and textualism, of an exclusive concern with the conceptual and discursive at the expense of more "practical" matters: "Deconstruction is not simply a matter of discourse or a matter of displacing the semantic content of the discourse, its conceptual structure or whatever. Deconstruction goes *through* certain social and political structures, meeting with resistance and displacing institutions as it does so . . . to deconstruct traditional sanctions—theoretical, philosophical, cultural—effectively, you have to displace . . . 'solid' structures, not only in the sense of material structures, but 'solid' in the sense of cultural, pedagogical, political, economic structures" ("In Discussion," 7–8). When the traditional sanctions are those of literary and cultural studies in the North American academy, the structures in question are solid indeed. But, as Derrida observes in "The Laws of Reflection: Nelson Mandela, in Admiration," force (including the force of deconstruction) presupposes resistance (13).

~

That the deconstructive impulse and its attendant institutional displacements have met and continue to meet with resistance is not news, not even to those whose knowledge of deconstruction is primarily as a journalistic phenomenon. The aggravated wartime scenario of the *Post* allegory also stamps the same newspaper's earlier reporting on deconstruction's incursion into the field of literary criticism. This time, the symptomatic article appeared not above the fold on page one but in the "Style" section of the Sunday edition. The headline reads, "War of the Words: A New Brand of Literary Criticism Has Scholars Everywhere Up in Arms," thus reprising a hyperbolic rhetoric of armed struggle that has characterized mainstream journalistic representations of deconstruction from the first.[4] Given its publication in the American capital's newspaper of record, whose readership includes those who make determinations on federal funding for scholarly research in the humanities, the account is not simply one among others, and it warrants commentary on grounds of its own positioning as well as the positions it rehearses.

Accompanying the feature is a half-page cartoon illustration that announces its generic affiliations: science fiction and horror. Crowned by sinister spaceships in the shape of graduation caps, the monstrous figure of a tweed-clad alien wreaks destruction on a campus turned terrordome, zapping hapless students with an unforgiving X-ray vision, all under the lurid banner "Humanities vs. the Deconstructionists." The lead paragraphs gloss the comic book graphics:

> It's the first horror movie about English teachers. It's called "The Beast From the Unfathomable" or, if you prefer, "Humanity vs. the Deconstructionists." It's in black-and-white and 2-D, but there are those who find it plenty scary just the same.
>
> The plot up to now:
>
> Alien spacecraft (rumored to bear the Air France emblem) have been sighted over college campuses from Yale to northern Alabama. Meanwhile, red-blooded young American scholars have begun speaking a strange language thick with words like "semiotics," "prosopopoeia," "apotropaic" and "diacritical."
>
> Attempts to treat the condition with bed rest and vitamin C have come to nought. (Lardner, "War of the Words," G1)

In the passage from the splashy banner to the fine print, "Humanities vs. the Deconstructionists," a formulation in which a disciplinary distinction is at stake, becomes "Humanity vs. the Deconstructionists," in which the future of the human race itself appears to be in jeopardy. (Given the disparity in order of magnitude between the two terms opposed in the second case, the question of what Washington policymakers call a "level playing field" arises; but of course the outcome of this war game has been decided in advance. Just let the "deconstructionists" try to overturn *this* opposition, to intervene in *this* field of forces.) The alarmist and xenophobic rhetoric first casts this threat to life as we know it as an invading force, which is readily metamorphosed into an infectious epidemic that defies conventional treatment (with overtones that are particularly sinister in the "age of AIDS").

The scenario then "Dissolve[s] to Cambridge, Mass.," presumptive location of the symbolic Centers for Disease Control and "headquarters of the national resistance to just about everything that has happened in the criticism and teaching of literature over the last 15 years, for a word from the resistance leader, Walter Jackson Bate, Kingsley Porter University Professor at Harvard." The report goes on to cite Bate's manifesto, "The Crisis in English Studies," an influential essay that deplores the academy's abandonment of the Renaissance concept of humane letters as a consequence of the "new ersatz specialism" and the increasing interest in and pursuit of theory in the "flagship of the humanistic fleet," English studies (Bate, "Crisis," 49, 46). What we are witnessing, in Bate's view, is "a wholesale reshuffling of values—a reshuffling downward, which is always easier than a reshuffling upward—down from the classical ideal of the central importance of literature to a self-imposed modesty and skepticism about its centrality" (49). According to the *Post*, "Bate's Paul Revere–like alarm, first sounded in Harvard Magazine, has been widely heard. 'I've never written anything that got so much in the way of correspondence,' says Bate, whose previous works include Pulitzer Prize–winning biographies of John Keats and Samuel Johnson." Bate's essay relies on a rhetoric of crisis likewise enlisted by such defenders of the traditional humanistic faith and upholders of cultural standards as René Wellek (in "Destroying Literary Studies," published in *The New Criterion*), Allan Bloom (in *The Closing of the American Mind*), and William Bennett (in his capacities as chairman of the National Endowment for the Humanities and secretary of education in the Reagan administration):[5] "The humanities are not merely entering, they are plunging into their worst state of crisis since the modern university was formed a century ago . . . the humanities are not only in the weakest state they ever suffered but seem bent on a self-destructive course, through a combination of anger, fear, and purblind defensiveness; the strongest help from enlightened administration in universities is indispensable to prevent the suicide (or, at least, self-trivialization) that will result" (46).

That the dimensions of the "crisis" are "not merely," "not only" ideological but institutional and political emerges in a call to battle that is strategically sounded: "My appeal is to administrations of universities and colleges, and also to alumni and educated people generally. It is often said that war is too important to leave to the generals—the 'experts.' So with the whole cultural heritage . . . that we call literature; it belongs to all of us. I couch this appeal in general terms, yet terms that are fairly specific when the cards are down and a tenure appointment is to be made, as it must be, every week throughout major universities in this country" (Bate, "Crisis," 52–53). Just as specific is the targeting of proponents and practitioners of "the strange stepchild of structuralism known as 'deconstructionism'"—as in the passages from "The Crisis in English Studies" selected for citation by the *Post*, in which Bate poses a version of the House subcommittee's question to the State Department official regarding the embassy incident: What price deconstruction?

> "At least a quarter of the profession acts as though it were intimidated," says Bate, by a "nihilistic view of literature, of human communication, and of life itself" [the latter an allusion to *Newsweek*'s early misreporting on deconstruction as "a decidedly nihilistic theory of life" (Woodward et al., "New Look," 82)]. He sees a trend that, unchecked, will "isolate literature still more into a self-sealed and autonomous entity, into which few students, few of the general public, indeed few—if any—writers of the past two thousand years could be able to enter or could wish to enter."
>
> . . . Bate and his allies indict deconstruction as nihilistic, whimsical, abstruse and incapable of distinguishing great literature from trash—and for spreading these maladies not only within the relatively small circle of avowed deconstructionists, but out among a far broader and more dangerous community of dupes and fellow-travelers. (Lardner, "War of the Words," G1, G10)

The *Post*'s characterization of deconstruction, an assemblage of quotations from Bate and other professors of the humanities, culminates in one whose morbid tonality belongs more properly to the obituary page than to the "Style" section: "'The long, solemn imposture of what passes for "modern literary theory" may now be reaching its point of turn,' writes Cambridge University's George Watson. 'Its more recent pronouncements, certainly, have a pale, autumnal air'" (Lardner, "War of the Worlds," G10). The clear and present danger to humanity and the humanities would seem to be subsiding.

One reason for the uniformity and familiarity—indeed, the almost rote quality—of these pronouncements about deconstruction may be the dense intrication of the professional academic's vested interest in discrediting a perceived challenge to established habits of thinking and teaching with a certain journalistic penchant for simplification and domestication, labeling and sloganeering (signaled in the reduction of the heterogeneous processes and effects of "deconstruction" to the axiomatics of "deconstructionism" or "deconstructivism"—a distinction that, as Derrida notes, "doesn't have the reality of a border which some would cross and others wouldn't. It is always being crossed, erased and retraced, retraced by being erased" ["Some Statements and Truisms," 75]).[6] Andrzej Warminski, among others, has analyzed

> the self-generating, balanced, closed economy of exchange that constitutes talk about deconstruction in America: an economy in which academics tell reporters what deconstruction is and then quote these reporters to tell other academics (and themselves) what it is, in which academics report to and report reporters, in which reporters report themselves—a self-contained informational relay system of self-reporting and self-quotation. . . . A contentless, meaningless, formalistic, nihilistic system if ever there was one—but, like all systems, terroristically coercive in policing its territory and enforcing its law. . . . What does this system have to contain? ("Deconstruction in America," 45)

Such a system—deconstruction's normalizing reappropriation by academic critics and journalists alike—makes for a very "solid" set of ideological and institutional structures. Within this framework, acoustic surveillance yields nothing new in the way of information (or intelligence)—only quotations of quotations of quotations that have the currency, and about the force, of gossip. What do these formulations tell us about the character and the effects of deconstruction's interventions in humanistic studies, and about the modes of resistance it has encountered?

~

Wherever it originates, the resistance in question may be most legible after the fact, and specifically as it is inscribed in a range of institutional effects. Deconstruction undertakes to counter such effects in kind, as well as to trace, in the institutionalization of literary and cultural theory in the North American academy, what may also be "the displaced symptoms of a resistance inherent in the theoretical enterprise itself" (de Man, "Resistance to Theory," 12).[7] The institutional determinations of the volume in which an earlier version of this chapter first appeared—it was commissioned by the Modern Language Association's Committee on Research and Publication to outline the transformations in literary studies in English over the past quarter century—suggest as one example of deconstruction's engagement with these resistances an essay commissioned for a comparable project roughly ten years earlier. At that time, Paul de Man was asked by the MLA's Committee on Research Activities (before it was incorporated, in a renegotiation of administrative boundaries, into the Publications Committee) to contribute the chapter on literary theory to a volume entitled *Introduction to Scholarship in Modern Languages and Literatures*. By his own account, de Man's submission, "Literary Theory: Aims and Methods," had difficulty meeting the well-defined scholarly and pedagogical criteria of such a volume, whose chapters "are expected to follow a clearly determined program: they are supposed to provide the reader with a select but comprehensive list of the main trends and publications in the field, to synthesize and classify the main problematic areas and to lay out a critical and programmatic projection of the solutions which can be expected in the foreseeable future. All this with a keen awareness that, ten years later, someone will be asked to repeat the same exercise" (de Man, "Resistance to Theory," 3). The essay, declined by the volume editors for its obvious failure to conform to these expectations, eventually appeared under the title "The Resistance to Theory." In it, de Man elaborates two orders of resistance that bear not only on the fate of his own efforts but more generally on deconstruction's impact on criticism and theory—on what we might, citing Geoffrey Hartman, call "the fate of reading."

The institutional resistances to theory and especially to deconstruction amount, in de Man's assessment, to a "resistance to the introduction of linguistic terminology in aesthetic and historical discourse about literature" ("Resistance to Theory," 12–13), a reaction motivated by ideological as well as professional investments in aestheticist and historicist approaches to texts. What de Man diagnoses, in response to Bate's "Crisis" essay, as a "return to philology" in contemporary theory coincides with his version of the deconstructive project, which he more often terms rhetorical reading, or simply reading. "Critical-linguistic analysis," closely tied to the descriptive sciences of philology and rhetoric, is in de Man's view a prerequisite for a genuine historical understanding of texts and for an effective critique of ideology. That is to say, the responsible account of a work of literature (or any textual instance) takes as its initial object of inquiry "not the meaning or the value but the modalities of production and of reception of meaning and of value prior to their establishment—the implication being that this establishment is problematic enough to warrant an autonomous discipline of critical investigation to consider its possibility and its status. Literary history, even when considered at the furthest remove from the platitudes of positivist historicism, is still the history of an understanding of which the possibility is taken for granted" ("Resistance to Theory," 7). In the North American context, deconstructive teaching thus takes place on ground prepared by the New Criticism in encouraging students "to begin by reading texts closely as texts and not to move at once into the general context of human experience or history" ("Resistance to Theory," 23) and training them to interrogate with some precision the ways in which meaning is constructed and conveyed before they zero in on the meaning itself—to take account, for example, of specific complications in the relation between the meaning and the order of words, between semantics and syntax. At the same time, deconstruction distinguishes itself from the New Criticism to the extent that it also "dislocates the borders, the framing of texts, everything which should preserve their immanence and make possible an internal reading or merely reading in the classical sense of the term" (Derrida, "Some Statements and Truisms," 86). Instead of being taught first of all as a vehicle for the received ideas that are often equated with traditional humanistic knowledge, literature "should be taught as a rhetoric and a poetics prior to being taught as a hermeneutics and a history" (de Man, "Resistance to Theory," 25–26). The first order of priority is "the difficulty and importance of engaging as rigorously as possible with language as a medium and model . . . the products of this order of engagement should be carefully differentiated rather than casually deplored" (Findlay, "Otherwise Engaged," 395).

De Man argues, for example, that one can go a long way in reading and teaching texts on the basis of "the most familiar and general of all linguistic models, the classical *trivium*" ("Resistance to Theory," 13). He invokes the tradition of humane letters that he is accused of abandoning to show how this model, "which considers the sciences of language as consisting of grammar, rhetoric and logic (or dialectics), is in fact a set of unresolved tensions powerful enough to have generated an infinitely prolonged discourse of endless frustration of which contemporary literary theory . . . is one more chapter" ("Resistance to Theory," 13). De Man's recollection of the contestatory relations among the categories of the *trivium* thus furnishes an instance of the memory work performed by deconstruction, of the way in which "the disruptive force of deconstruction is always already contained within the architecture of the work" (Derrida, "Art of Memoires," 73). A reconsideration of the *trivium* in light of its configuration of the several functions of language (and the disciplines to which they give rise) brings to light a hierarchical order whereby grammar has been assumed to be at the service of logic, which has in turn been posited as the link between the sciences of language and the sciences of the phenomenal world. The troublesome potential of rhetoric in this scenario is particularly evident in the case of the literary text, which "foregrounds the rhetorical over the grammatical and the logical function" of language (de Man, "Resistance to Theory," 14). De Man would have the reader resist the tendency to preempt analysis by reducing the literary text to extralinguistic, extratextual conditions, a resistance effected pedagogically by teaching students how to read language as rhetoric and as writing.

In de Man's reinscription of the term, "reading" as the pragmatic and hence unpredictable engagement with the specifics of language as an open-ended rhetorical and grammatological construct is the locus of a second-order resistance: that of the reading (the deconstructive) operation itself to codification as method, to formalization as technique, to systematization as theory. "Mere reading, it turns out, prior to any theory, is able to transform critical discourse in a manner that would appear deeply subversive to those who think of the teaching of literature as a substitute for the teaching of theology, ethics, psychology, or intellectual history" (de Man, "Return to Philology," 24). The radicality of reading as practiced and taught by de Man undoes language (especially but not only literary language) as a stable epistemological ground:

> [R]eading disrupts the continuity between the theoretical and the phenomenal and thus forces a recognition of the incompatibility of language and intuition. Since the latter constitutes the foundational basis of cognition upon which perception, consciousness, experience and the logic and the understanding, not to mention the aesthetics that are attendant to them, are constructed, there results a wholesale shakeout in the organization and conceptualization of knowledge, from which language, conceived as a double system of tropes and persuasion, that is as a rhetorical entity, emerges as the unavoidable dimensionality of all cognition. (Godzich, "Tiger," x)

To the extent that it engages language as "a disruptive intertwining of trope and persuasion or—which is not quite the same thing—of cognitive and performative language" (de Man, Preface to *Allegories*, ix), reading thus problematizes not only literature's aesthetic function (i.e., the presumed compatibility of linguistic structures with aesthetic values), but the very category of the aesthetic conceived since Kant as the articulation of pure with practical reason, of cognition with action. De Man's own readings of Kant's *Critique of Judgment* and Hegel's *Aesthetics* seek to interrogate (rather than take for granted) the possibility of a passage from the epistemological to the ethical and political domains by elaborating the ways in which, in the long wake of Schiller's domesticating interpretation, "[a]esthetic judgment came to be replaced or overlaid by an ideological construct of values, now commonly taken to be the aesthetic, even though, de Man insists, the underlying judgment will not support such an overlay but will actively work to dismantle it. Only an activity such as reading can come in touch with this process and experience the resistance of the material to the ideological overlay" (Godzich, "Tiger," xi).

It remains briefly to account for the way in which, in a further turn of the theoretical screw, the "return to philology" has come around, in turn, to a so-called "return to history." Well before the self-denomination and self-institution of the new historicism (and its attendant "new politicism"), de Man sketched the conditions of its advent:

> We speak as if, with the problems of literary form resolved once and forever, and with the techniques of structural analysis refined to near perfection, we could now move "beyond formalism" towards the questions that really interest us and reap, at last, the fruits of the ascetic concentration on techniques that prepared us for this decisive step. With the internal law and order of literature well policed, we can now confidently devote ourselves to the foreign affairs, the external politics of literature. ("Semiology and Rhetoric," 3)

While the terms of de Man's analogy ironically reverse the order of priorities invoked in the name of national interest since the end of the Cold War, much recent work in literary and cultural theory would indeed seem to mark a swerving away from reading (again, often misleadingly cast as aestheticism or textualism, as a "nostalgia for an unadulterated and uncontaminated Ur-text beyond the blemish of interpretation and history" [Gasché, Introduction, xiv]), and a return to questions, in Frank Lentricchia's phrase, of "criticism and social change," of literature's historical status and political effects—in some cases, as if this status and these effects could be determined apart from, in the absence of, the insights afforded by reading. As a priority of the historicist turn has come the call, held by some to be long overdue, to historicize deconstruction itself, to contextualize and periodize a movement that has sought to question the validity of such an unproblematic return and recovery, particularly when it circumvents reading in favor of a more immediate invocation or thematization of history. Although the historical situating and self-situating of deconstruction are imperative, its historicizing has too often meant "playing the overall boring game which consists in applying the most worn-out schemes of the history of ideas to the specificity of what is happening now," a game whose moves include consolidating and closing off the heterogeneity of deconstructive operations into a totalizing theory, a set of theorems and theses: "deconstructionism" (Derrida, "Some Statements and Truisms," 79). As Derrida goes on to note, "the most recent and most interesting developments of Marxism and of what is called new historicism . . . institute themselves in reaction to a deconstructionist poststructuralism which is itself *either* nothing but a figure or a stabilizing reappropriation of deconstruction *or else* a caricatural myth projected by Marxists and new historicists out of self interest or misunderstanding" (90). To the extent that an overly impatient "return to history" may overlook deconstruction's differences from deconstructionism, its resistances to reappropriation in historicist terms—and to the extent that it forgets the irreducible textuality of history and histories—it risks positing nonreading in a systematic way. When the avoidance of reading becomes systematic, hegemonic, then reading in the sense posited by deconstruction, however circumscribed its apparent scope, becomes a counterhegemonic undertaking, one that may prove crucial to any effective transformation of the institutions in, for, and against which we work.[8]

§ 2 The work to come

(Journalism's intervention in a theoretical corpus)

Something crisis-like was taking place at that moment, making practices and assumptions problematic that had been taken for granted.

—Paul de Man, "Criticism and Crisis"

By most accounts, the disclosure of Paul de Man's wartime journalism precipitated something of a "crisis"; the term recurs insistently in what is by now a host of reflections on the import, theoretical and political, of those early texts. In "Blindness and Hindsight," one of 38 essays collected in *Responses: On Paul de Man's Wartime Journalism*, Catherine Gallagher notes the way in which this crisis scenario dovetails with recent mainstream press reports of "the failure of the humanities in general and literary studies in particular"—an ongoing journalistic narrative, alarmist in tone, that casts theory as a kind of invading force on the cultural landscape (204). That story, of course, is traceable to academic sources, indebted to a rhetoric of crisis generated by some within the profession who take theory—by which they most often mean deconstruction—to be a threat to established habits of thought and what are called traditional values. As the previous chapter recalls, among the professors of literature who have gone on record as deploring theory's incursion into the humanistic disciplines, Walter Jackson Bate led the way with his manifesto "The Crisis in English Studies," published in *Harvard Magazine* in 1982. Bate's claim is that "The humanities are not merely entering, they are plunging into their worst state of crisis since the modern university was formed a century ago. . . . the humanities are not only in the weakest state they ever suffered but seem bent on a self-destructive course" (Bate,

"Crisis," 46). And he indicts "the strange stepchild of structuralism known as 'deconstructionism,'" a "nihilistic view of literature, of human communication, and of life itself," as chiefly responsible for the current crisis. As Gallagher rightly discerns, "The discovery that de Man had written for a collaborationist journal fit beautifully into this story because it provided a perfect symmetry between the beginning and the end. Deconstruction was no longer just the harbinger of outrages against humanity; it actually originated in such outrages. The outcome could no longer be in doubt because it was contained in the original" ("Blindness and Hindsight," 204). In these terms, the disclosure of the wartime writings could elicit a collective "I told you so" from critics as well as journalists long incensed by deconstruction's impact within and beyond the academy.

In one of the first substantive reviews of *Wartime Journalism, 1939–1943* and *Responses: On Paul de Man's Wartime Journalism*, Lynne Higgins complicates this symmetrical narrative of origins and ends, even as she too adopts the rhetoric of crisis: "Reading the two volumes together," she writes, "gives one a sense of the current identity crisis within literary studies. The de Man 'affair' did not *create* that crisis, but it does magnify the complexities and raise the stakes" (Review, 105–6). For critics whose stake in the matter may amount in great part to self-interest, to fear for the possibility of their own contamination through the operative "logic of transmission," "Protection consists of mastering continuities and constructing distances. . . . It is the very indirect and mediated nature of the degrees of collaboration that makes it terrifying. The identity crisis takes the form of an urgent question: is the work I'm doing complicitous with something I would be horrified to be associated with?" In times of crisis—Higgins here invokes the AIDS pandemic, not simply as an analogy—"we have to know who we are sleeping with. We want 'safe criticism'" (Review, 110).

The texts comprising the wartime journalism—a heterogeneous corpus including contributions to the Belgian dailies *Le Soir* and *Het Vlaamsche Land* and the monthly *Bibliographie Dechenne*, all issued under the control of the occupation authorities, as well as to *Jeudi* and the *Cahiers du Libre Examen*, the weekly newspaper and monthly journal of the socialist student circle at the Université Libre de Bruxelles, published prior to the occupation—were themselves written out of what the young Paul de Man repeatedly diagnosed as a crisis, one whose dimensions were manifold. In "A la recherche d'un nouveau mode d'expression," a review of Charles Dekeukeleire's *L'Emotion sociale* originally published in *Le Soir* in March 1942 (a month in which, as the detailed chronology compiled by the editors of *Responses* notes, "German military authorities institute obligatory labor service for some categories of workers" [xvi], and in which *Le Soir*, with an average daily circulation of 255,000, is the most widely read periodical in the country [xvii]), de Man advises his readers that "The military events, as gigantic and full of consequence as they are, cannot make us forget that at the same time a crisis of a spiritual order is proceeding whose historic import is incalculable" ("A la recherche," 208). And allusions such as that to the "particularly delicate crisis that a man passes through around his twentieth year" ("Le problème de l'adolescence," 246, originally published in *Le Soir* on June 30, 1942) suggest that the spiritual crisis concomitant with the ongoing political upheaval had an autobiographical dimension as well. This rhetoric of crisis, sustained in many of the young journalist's contributions to *Le Soir* and *Het Vlaamsche Land*, is harnessed to a logic that argues collaboration to be a pragmatic, indeed a necessary, response to the current state of affairs, to the force of facts, of history: "There thus emerges the demonstration of that ineluctable truth of history," he writes in July 1942 in a review of the second volume of Alfred Fabre-Luce's *Journal de la France*: "the politics of collaboration results from the present situation not as an ideal desired by all of the people but as an irresistible necessity which none can escape, even if he thinks he ought to move in another direction" ("Journal de la France," 253; see also the review of Jacques Chardonne's *Voir la figure*, 158–59, originally published in *Le Soir* on October 28, 1941). In "Qu'est-ce qu'un collaborateur?" Sartre identifies this logic (and ideologic) as that of realism. Elaborating the significance of Sartre's insight, Werner Hamacher observes that

> the ideology of realism, identified as a central element of collaboration, is itself a danger to democratically organized societies. The pragmatism, positivism and historicism which have long been a part of the ideological profile of democracies can hardly be regarded as anything other than variants of that realism which finds the final guarantee of reality in the power of so-called facts. This reality is actually first generated by all sorts of societal—and not only societal—institutions and all sorts of techniques—among them techniques of language. . . . It is in realism that Sartre marks the point of complicity between democratic and fascist systems. Putting this realism into question is an eminently political act, even if it is not articulated in explicitly political terms, but rather in linguistic and philological ones (as, for example, in de Man's later writings). No one with a critical mind will be startled that the institutions of this ideological realism try to denounce any such questioning as an attack on the basic foundations of 'Western values.' ("Journals, Politics," 448)

Nor should it come as a surprise that the denunciations are couched in the rhetoric of crisis.

In the aftermath of the archival discovery that brought de Man's earliest publications once again to light, the crisis translates, especially for those indebted to his later writing and teaching, as a need, an imperative, to make sense of an event that has disrupted working premises and practices. Perhaps the event-character of the disclosure of the wartime journalism, which in the view of Samuel Weber and other commentators administered "a shock and an intensity in direct proportion to the influence of [de Man's] work and to the respect inspired by his person" (Weber, "Monument Disfigured," 410), might best be thought not so much as a contingent bibliographical find, but rather on the model of a missive, an open letter—or letter bomb—delivered after long delay. Barbara Johnson speculates that "Whether or not those articles contributed in any way to the wartime history of Belgium, the arrival of this long-delayed letter strikes us *now* with the full disruptive force of an event. It is an event that is structured *like* what de Man describes as an 'occurrence'—an irreversible disruption of cognition." But in this case, she goes on to specify, "it is a disruption that is happening *to* his own acts of cognition. It is as though de Man had tried to theorize"—after the fact, in the mature work—"the disruption"—before the fact, in and by the precritical if not pretheoretical journalism—"of his own acts of theorizing, had tried to include the theory's own outside within it. But that theory's outside was precisely, we now know, always already within. And he could not, of course, control the very loss of control he outlined as inevitable and defined as irony. . . . The arrival of this purloined letter, then, is an event not only for de Man but also for his readers, however uncannily his theory might have predicted its inevitability" (Johnson, "Preface to the Paperback Edition," xii). Johnson's account credits de Man's late essays—she quotes the 1983 lecture "Kant and Schiller," but could as well have cited "Hypogram and Inscription," "Anthropomorphism and Trope in the Lyric," "Aesthetic Formalization in Kleist," or "Phenomenality and Materiality in Kant"—with a reflection on the nature of historical occurrence, and specifically on its accessibility to cognition, that makes a particular claim on our attempts to come to terms with the explosive event at hand, the belated disclosure of the abandoned writings. More generally, she helps to focus the question of the continuing importance of de Man's mature work not only for "the epistemological analysis of what 'reality' is and how it de-constitutes itself in the tensions of language" (Hamacher, "Journals, Politics," 454), but also and especially "for any analysis of the totalitarian impulse insofar as it transmits itself in texts," "for the historico-political analysis of textuality in general," as "an effective analysis of historical acts [and, one might add, events, occurrences] which are dissociated from cognition by language" (Kamuf, "Impositions," 225).

Other formulations in *Responses* explore the pertinence of de Man's analysis of the dissociation of cognition from performance on the one hand and from what he termed "the materiality of actual history" on the other. A number of these employ blindness as a figure for the disruption, the failure of cognition in the face of the event. As against Gallagher's summary assessment that "Hindsight has revised nothing and confirmed everything" ("Blindness and Hindsight," 207), Cynthia Chase writes that "After the emergence of de Man's 1940–42 articles, one necessarily writes about his writing differently than before—insofar as one writes about a subject they do not as such address, about an occurrence they do not see. The reappearance of those abandoned texts is something that happens to de Man's writing from the outside"—an "outside" that, as Johnson observes, was always already within, which is to say it is not so much an outside as a before—"which thus strikes it with blindness with regard to what is nevertheless its own situation, or rather ours, that of his students, readers. Here for the first time indubitably is an occurrence pertinent to his writing which it cannot see and about which it has nothing to say. But at the same time it says a great deal about just that predicament—the blindness of writing; and also—but why is it only now that one learns to read this?—about the implication of thought and writing in the violence of history, and particularly that European 20th-century violence, Nazism." Chase's argument, grounded in a meticulous reading and rereading of the journalism as well as the theoretical work, is not only that de Man's late essays on the aesthetic ideology (in particular "Aesthetic Formalization in Kleist") are crucial for thinking "the complicities of modes of education and models of history with the fascist totalitarian state" but also that "these writings' not knowing, not seeing their circumstances—which is not a matter of repressing or concealing—is a key dimension of what they give us to read" (Chase, "Trappings," 44). Reading, our reading, must account for the blindness, for the critical failure of cognition to inscribe a certain history.

In "Edges of Understanding," Rodolphe Gasché has recourse to the same figuration in characterizing the severe shortcomings of the early journalism: "the essays of *Het Vlaamsche Land* and *Le Soir* do not show de Man to have sensed the catastrophic danger that Nazi Germany represented not only with respect to the Jewish people, but to the whole of Europe and the celebrated values of Western civilization as well. This is rather difficult to understand today, after the fact. But if de Man did not come to grips with the horror that was in the offing, it was *among other things* because his analytical apparatus did not provide the means to capture the viciousness and aberration of the Nazi endeavor *on all fronts*" (215). (As Hamacher specifies, "Despite the control [the articles] exercise over it, the vocabulary of the time is virtually never scrutinized or redefined" ["Journals, Politics," 438].) And Gasché concludes that, if the young de Man's "intellectual instruments (like those of most of his contemporaries, and of many present intellectuals as well)" kept him from a precise understanding of events, "It was left to the later de Man to systematically put into question all those blinding schemes, categories and concepts by means of which he had, in his journalistic writings, unsuccessfully tried to gain insight into the political situation in Belgium in the early forties" ("Edges of Understanding," 215).

Among the most suggestive accounts of what it is that the event of the disclosure summons us to read and to think is Geoffrey Hartman's, in "Looking Back on Paul de Man," his two-part contribution to *Reading de Man Reading* (the essay's first part was written before, and the second after, the wartime journalism came to light). "By an irony that deserves a name of its own," he writes, "the disclosure of the early articles imbeds a biographical fact in our consciousness that tends to devour all other considerations. It may not spare the later achievement, whose intellectual power we continue to feel." We continue to feel, for example, the force of de Man's theorization of the blindness of writing, the limits of criticism and self-criticism. "One could argue," Hartman pursues, "that there is no relation between the young journalist, age twenty-one, and the distinguished theorist who published his first book at age fifty-one. Or that what relation obtains is one of reaction formation, as when he accuses Husserl of blindly privileging 'European supremacy' at the very time (1935) that Europe 'was about to destroy itself as center in the name of an unwarranted claim to be the center.' For de Man too was a European who 'escaped from the necessary self-criticism that is prior to all philosophical truth about the self.'" But, Hartman is careful to add, "what we are seeing here"—always allowing for our own blindness—"is a special case of what happens all the time. A new fact, often a new text, makes a difference in the way we read. Although history has moved more quickly in this case, we are always in the situation of having to revise our judgment of a work, however monumental it once appeared to be" ("Looking Back," 18).

It is no accident that the recurrent topoi that organize these responses to the wartime journalism—criticism and crisis, blindness and insight, irony and history among them—should be drawn from de Man's theoretical legacy. In particular, these formulations redirect us to *Blindness and Insight* and to its opening essay "Criticism and Crisis," first published in 1967, where de Man interrogates the "recurrent epistemological structure that characterizes all statements made in the mood and the rhetoric of crisis" (de Man, "Criticism and Crisis," 14). As Hartman recalls, that analysis enlists ("[f]or reasons of economy") "an example from philosophy," the 1935 lectures that would later become Husserl's *The Crisis of the European Sciences and Transcendental Phenomenology* and their "description of philosophy as a process by means of which naive assumptions are made accessible to consciousness by an act of critical self-understanding. Husserl conceived of philosophy primarily as a self-interpretation by means of which we eliminate what he calls *Selbstverhülltheit*, the tendency of the self to hide from the light it can cast on itself. The universality of philosophical knowledge stems from a persistently reflective attitude that can take philosophy itself for its theme" (de Man, "Criticism and Crisis," 15). But when Husserl's reader, "[a]lerted by this convincing appeal to self-critical vigilance," is led to apply the philosopher's standard to the very text in which it is established, that text is found wanting in its own terms, above all when it claims philosophy as "the historical privilege of European man":

> Husserl speaks repeatedly of non-European cultures as primitive, prescientific and pre-philosophical, myth-dominated and congenitally incapable of the disinterested distance without which there can be no philosophical meditation. This, although by his own definition philosophy, as unrestricted reflection upon the self, necessarily tends toward a universality that finds its concrete, geographical correlative in the formation of supratribal, supranational communities such as, for instance, Europe. Why this geographical expansion should have chosen to stop, once and forever, at the Caucasus, Husserl does not say. . . .

> The privileged viewpoint of the post-Hellenic, European consciousness is never for a moment put into question; the crucial, determining examination on which depends Husserl's right to call himself, by his own terms, a philosopher, is in fact never undertaken. As a European, it seems that Husserl escapes from the necessary self-criticism that is prior to all philosophical truth about the self. . . . Husserl's claim to European supremacy hardly stands in need of criticism today. Since we are speaking of a man of superior good will, it suffices to point to the pathos of such a claim at a moment when Europe was about to destroy itself as center in the name of its unwarranted claim to be the center. (de Man, "Criticism and Crisis," 15–16)

Writing "in what was in fact a state of urgent personal and political crisis about a more general form of crisis," Husserl unwittingly exemplifies what de Man takes to be "the structure of all crisis-determined statements. . . . The rhetoric of crisis states its own truth in the mode of error. It is itself radically blind to the light it emits," to the insight it makes possible (de Man, "Criticism and Crisis," 16). Husserl thus joins the ranks of thinkers in whose critical practice de Man discerns a cognitive mechanism figured as blindness and insight. Ably summarizing and situating de Man's analysis, its theoretical and potentially its institutional consequences, Wlad Godzich writes:

> the blindness, far from being disabling, was constitutive of the insight, yet nonetheless remained a blindness to the person affected with it. It was this predicament of critical activity that led de Man to formulate a more properly theoretical stance in which the mechanism of blindness and insight would be understood without being disabled, or at least not in such a way as to render further insights impossible. De Man's solicitude in the preservation of the mechanism has something profoundly disquieting, if not downright scandalous, about it. Our impulse, bred in the bone by several centuries of education, is to correct an error when we come across it. De Man's willingness to let it be marked a profound break with a major component of the Western cognitive tradition, one that is the motor of the disciplines, especially the scientific ones. ("Religion," 155; see also Graff, "Looking Past," 249).

By way of his reading of Husserl's text, then, de Man is led to ask: "How does this pattern of self-mystification that accompanies the experience of crisis apply to literary criticism? Husserl was demonstrating the urgent philosophical necessity of putting the privileged European standpoint into question, but remained himself entirely blind to this necessity, behaving in the most unphilosophical way possible at the very moment when he rightly understood the primacy of philosophical over empirical knowledge. He was, in fact, stating the privileged status of philosophy as an authentic language, but withdrawing at once from the demands of this authenticity as it applied to himself" (16–17). In "The Monument Disfigured," Weber glosses de Man's account: "De Man's 'point' . . . is that the notion of self-criticism, with reference to which Husserl seeks to define the specificity of Western philosophy, itself depends upon a highly contradictory set of assumptions which themselves may well comprise the enabling limit of 'criticism' itself (and which hence would have to remain uncriticized and uncriticizable). These assumptions have to do with Husserl's use of the term 'European' to define and determine the philosophical attitude of self-criticism he is engaged in defending against the crisis that has befallen it." In Weber's assessment, then, "the question raised by de Man with respect to Husserl (in both senses of that phrase)[1] involves the status of *criticism* itself, and concomitantly, the problem of judgment, that is, of proceeding from the particular (European man) to the general (the universal validity of the self-critical attitude of philosophical thought)"—this inscription of the particular in the general being for de Man "the purpose of any cognition" (de Man, "Aesthetic Formalization," 276). "What is at stake in this problem," as Weber makes plain, "is the relation of thinking to alterity, to the others: here, the non-European. The question de Man is raising is that of self-limitation, of *demarcation*. . . . the point . . . is that the 'spiritual' generalization of European humanity in order to define a norm of thought valid beyond the limits of the European continent, requires necessarily the exclusion and subordination of other cultures"[2] (Weber, "Monument Disfigured," 408).

How then, if at all, are we to bring to bear on de Man's own history, on the grave pattern of self-mystification inscribed in the wartime writings, the lesson for which Husserl serves (the later de Man) as example? Do the terms and distinctions afforded in the theoretical work indeed make a particular claim on our efforts to render intelligible its relation to the early journalism, a claim that we ignore or reject at the expense of a better understanding? If we attend to the passage in which de Man locates the operation of blindness and insight in Husserl's text ("Husserl was demonstrating the urgent philosophical necessity of putting the privileged European standpoint into question, but remained himself entirely blind to this necessity, behaving in the most unphilosophical way possible at the very moment when he rightly understood the primacy of philosophical over empirical knowledge" [de Man, "Criticism and Crisis," 16]), we find that much of the burden of the argument falls on the sense or senses of "demonstrating," among them, according to the *Oxford English Dictionary*, "proving beyond the possibility of doubt by a process of argument or logical deduction" by way of a line of reasoning that can close with *quid est demonstrandum*. The analysis of Husserl's demonstration thus yields a logic of blindness and insight, based on the principle of noncontradiction, that seems sufficient to his case, since the "blindness"—unphilosophical behavior—and the "insight"—right understanding—occur "*at the very [same] moment*," since "[h]e was, in fact, stating the privileged status of philosophy as an authentic language but withdrawing *at once* from the demands of this authenticity as it applied to himself" (de Man, "Criticism and Crisis," 16–17). The simultaneity that marks the operation of the logic, the law of blindness and insight in Husserl's text might seem to promise the possibility of a dialectical mediation of the two terms, but it is nonetheless "against any dialectical reappropriation or synthesis of blindness and insight that de Man is waging his most explicit, powerful attacks. In trying to define the relation of blindness and insight, he insists: 'The contradictions, however, can never cancel each other out, nor do they enter into the synthesizing dynamics of a dialectic' (*Blindness and Insight*, 102)" (Klein, "Blindness of Hyperboles," 36; Klein cites de Man's essay "The Rhetoric of Blindness").

The impossibility of a dialectical resolution is all the more emphatic in de Man's own case. If we "apply de Man's statement about Husserl's claim to European supremacy to the writer of 'Inhoud der Europeesche gedachte'" (de Graef, "Aspects," 119), we find that the de Manian corpus resists the imposition of the categories of blindness and insight conceived according to a logic that dictates their mutual cancellation or dialectical synthesis. For the two textual conditions do not occur simultaneously, are not co-present in this body of work, but are separated by more than a quarter century. In these terms, a decisive difference between Husserl's case and de Man's—a difference that de Man's late writings help us to read—is that in the latter the temporal dimension is not contingent but constitutive.[3]

The stakes—and the eventual outcome—of the crisis to which the disclosure of the wartime journalism has given rise thus depend upon the possible articulation of the early texts with the later ones, as a reading of *Responses* makes clear.[4] Gasché writes that "undoubtedly, it is the relation, the absence of a relation, or something other than a relation . . . between the early journalism and de Man's mature work that represents the most interesting problem . . . no analysis of what is to be related, of the *sort of relation that is possible, in the first place, between the relata,* seems to have been undertaken" ("Edges of Understanding," 215–16). "De Man's early writings . . . are a far cry from what he was later to become involved in, and thus it is no small task to demonstrate any *significant* relation between the two corpuses" ("Edges of Understanding," 217). In Derrida's formulation, the task is specifically "to articulate [the wartime journalism] with the work to come while avoiding, if possible, two more or less symmetrical errors": that of declaring "no relation, sealed frontier between the two, absolute heterogeneity" and that of "amalgam, continuism, analogism, teleologism, hasty totalization, reduction and derivation" (Derrida, "Like the Sound," 151), of "asserting complete identity, as though discontinuity and history were a mere ruse or epiphenomenon"

(Weber, "Monument Disfigured," 410). An articulation that would do justice to such a history—and to history as such—must first pass by way of a thinking of temporality, a reading of the relation of past to present that presumes neither a ready symmetry between them nor their linking by way of a homogenizing narrative of origins and ends.

If we begin by rereading the conceptual metaphors of blindness and insight in light of the intervention of time that renders the terms radically asymmetrical, we find that the sense of "demonstrating" as the working out of an argument or a logical deduction yields to a more properly rhetorical (and practical) sense: that of the demonstration *effect* of the *example*. In these terms, Husserl was blindly offering himself as an example of blindness (the figure, again, for his unphilosophical behavior) "at the very moment" when he was stating his insight into the superiority of philosophical over empirical knowledge.[5] And in de Man's case, the wartime writings could be understood in part to serve as examples—in advance—of the (precritical, ideological) blindness that the later (critical, theoretical) insight will expose, so unsparingly, as such.[6] This economy of the example would not be subsumable under any logic or dialectic. Neither before nor after the fact can one control or fully account for one's own (or another's) status as example, with its unpredictable effects of meaning and of force.[7]

Reflection on the demonstration effect of the example also prompts active consideration of the question of how occupied Belgium remains an example *for us*—a question that may be overlooked if our response to the disclosure of the wartime writings takes the tempting form of simple condemnation. As Hartman writes in "History and Judgment," "Denunciation, at this point, is not enough; it tends to foster a paranoid style of localizing evil that removes the issues too far from our time" (69). "Mere reactions," concurs Hamacher, "are powerless, especially when dealing with the discourse of totalitarianism. . . . Elements of totalitarian ideologies live on—and most stubbornly in those who proclaim their own immunity" ("Journals, Politics," 466–67). The question of how the then and there chronicled by the young journalist may implicate us, here and now, poses the challenge of thinking history, not as a totalizing narrative of symmetrical origins and ends, but in the precise terms of the material specificity of the event: "'History,' this vague abstraction, seems then and now to function as a powerful means of homogenizing and making a taboo out of history—namely *that* history which exists only concretely, singularly, idiosyncratically, painfully. To judge history on the basis of its empty generality is to deny the past its particularities, and to run the risk of repeating it in its worst traits" (Hamacher, "Journals, Politics," 463). This is a risk we can hardly afford to run unawares—that is to say, blindly.

~

> Doch lies nur, lies!
>
> —Goethe, *Die Wahlverwandtschaften*

> [T]he gift of an ordeal, the summons to a work of reading, of historical interpretation, of ethical-political reflection—an interminable analysis well beyond the sequence 1940–42. In the future and for the future. . . .
>
> —Derrida, "Like the Sound of the Sea Deep Within a Shell: Paul de Man's War"

Rather than resorting to empty generalities, paraphrasing and summarizing the heterogeneous arguments of the wartime journalism as well as those of the responses to them, we may do better (not only "for reasons of economy") to explore these questions on the basis of an example—one of the few—of a text that de Man engaged in both his early and later work in order to posit a possible articulation of the two and to substantiate what we have alluded to as his own blindness and insight. The example is Goethe's *Die Wahlverwandtschaften* (*The Elective Affinities*), whose French translation de Man reviewed in *Le Soir* in May 1942 under the title "Universalisme de Goethe." He undertook to analyze the novel again more than 40 years later in a lecture for "Reading and Rhetorical Structures," a course he taught in the Literature Major at Yale University in the spring of 1983; the late lecture is thus contemporaneous with his readings of Kant, Schiller, and Kleist and their elaboration of his analysis of aesthetic ideology.[8] In it, de Man radically revises his former judgment of Goethe's text.

Before engaging the terms of de Man's commentaries on the novel, early and late, we might recollect a passage in which Goethe's text itself speaks to circumstances akin to those of the disclosure of the wartime journalism. In the novel's ninth chapter, the laying of the foundation stone for the new summerhouse is marked with an elaborate ceremony featuring an address by the mason on the importance of his own craft for the architectural project, which, "if it be not done in concealment, yet must pass into concealment" (Goethe, *Elective Affinities*, 66).

> But as the man who commits some evil deed has to fear, that, notwithstanding all precautions, it will one day come to light—so too must he expect who has done some good thing in secret, that it also, in spite of himself, will appear in the day; and therefore we make this foundation stone at the same time a stone of memorial [*Deswegen machen wir diesen Grundstein zugleich zum Denkstein*]. Here, in these various hollows which have been hewn into it, many things are now to be buried, as a witness to some far-off world [*Zeugnis für eine entfernte Nachwelt*]—these metal cases hermetically sealed contain documents in writing [*schriftliche Nachrichten*]; matters of various note are engraved on these plates; in these fair glass bottles we bury the best old wine, with a note of the year of its vintage. We have coins too of many kinds, from the mint of the current year. . . . There is space yet remaining, if guest or spectator desires to offer anything to the afterworld. . . . But in that we bury this treasure together with [the foundation stone], we do it in the remembrance—in this most enduring of works—of the perishableness of human things. We remember [*wir denken uns eine Möglichkeit*] that a time may come when this cover so fast sealed shall again be lifted. (*Elective Affinities*, English 65–66; German 66–67)[9]

The written documents (*Nachrichten*, news reports, literally, "after-accounts") sealed in this time capsule—which is always potentially a time bomb—share an affinity with de Man's wartime journalism: Both are emphatically of their time in their referential function, but both reemerge at a future date, like the long-delayed letter (arriving, now, from before and beyond the grave), coming to light for what Hamacher terms "their second phase of use" ("Journals, Politics," 438).

In the concluding entry in his "Journals, Politics," one of the most consequential essays in *Responses* for thinking history as of the order of events and their possible articulation, Hamacher cites de Man's *Le Soir* review: "On May 26, 1942 de Man writes—under the title 'Universalisme de Goethe,' a discussion of Goethe's *Wahlverwandtschaften*—several sentences which are not written by an ideologue, a tactician in a politico-literary battle, or an accomplice of the collaborationist press, but by a *reader*. The other sentences must not be forgotten; these should be remembered as well. They concern the 'strange interlude' in the middle of the novel, in the early chapters of the second section, during which 'absolutely nothing happens which would advance the development of the drama'" ("Journals, Politics," 467). He goes on to translate de Man's text:

> There has been a great deal of discussion about the appropriateness of these pages, which seem unbearably long to some. And yet, they constitute one of the most alluring and original parts of the whole work.(. . .) It seems, though, that their principal *raison d'être* is the introduction into the novel of the factor of time, of the *duration* [de Man's emphasis] of events. Reality never presents itself as an uninterrupted movement towards a dénouement: it marks the stopping times [*temps d'arrêt*] during which, under the empire of inertia or human automatism, entirely eventless periods unroll their monotonous uniformity. A narrative which aims to produce the real rhythm of existence must insert such epochs. . . . the interlude in the *Wahlverwandtschaften* is certainly one of the most successful attempts of this kind. (de Man, "Universalisme de Goethe," 238)[10]

In attending to the economy of memory and forgetting crucial to our responses to these texts, Hamacher is right to mark, with emphasis, the distinction between de Man as an ideologue and as a reader: Both play a role in the not altogether homogeneous corpus of the wartime journalism. Specifically, the youthful ideologue and tactician is a mouthpiece for what the later theorist and reader would target under the rubric of aesthetic ideology. The pursuit of the latter project necessarily passes by way of what de Man terms "critical-linguistic analysis" ("Interview," 121), including, importantly, a sustained investigation of the values associated, at least since the late eighteenth century, with symbolic and allegorical conceptions of language. With reference to Goethe, Schiller, and Schelling, as well as to Coleridge, de Man argues that the symbol, predicated on the assumed continuity and simultaneity of "the sensory image and the supersensory totality that the image suggests," in turn grounds an understanding of the subject–object relation "in which the experience of the object takes on the form of a perception or a sensation. The ultimate intent of the image is synthesis," and "the mode of this synthesis is defined as symbolic by the priority conferred on the initial moment of sensory perception"—that is, on the *aesthetic* moment ("Rhetoric of Temporality," 189, 193). The symbol, then, proves to be the linguistic condition of possibility of "a certain claim for the autonomy and the power of the aesthetic which is being asserted in the wake of Schiller, but not necessarily in the wake of Kant"—that is, aesthetic ideology (de Man, "Kant and Schiller," 131). Allegory, in de Man's reading, disrupts the possibility of the symbolic synthesis by opening up a constitutive temporal dimension, the difference that divides the allegorical sign from the previous sign to which it refers. Allegory confesses the failure of coincidence forgotten or repressed in the model of the symbol, in which the relationship of image and substance is taken to be "one of simultaneity, which, in truth, is spatial in kind, and in which the intervention of time is merely a matter of contingency" (de Man, "Rhetoric of Temporality," 207). In its detail and its scope, this analysis effects a radical revision of the conventional literary–historical and aesthetic categories through which we read romanticism (and idealism), the same categories that are in full force in de Man's early review of *The Elective Affinities.*

In the review's first paragraph, the spirit of Goethe is said to be "independent of the conditions of space and time," and the novel, "one of Goethe's most perfect works," to be "the living image of the universalism of its author" ("Universalisme de Goethe," 238). De Man's assertion that there is nothing in or about the novel "that doesn't seem to us essentially modern" stands as an awkward antecedent to the claim in his late essay on "Aesthetic Formalization in Kleist" that, "for all the attention it has received," the text on the marionette theater (published in 1810, and thus virtually contemporaneous with Goethe's novel, which appeared in 1809) has nonetheless "remained curiously unread and enigmatic" and "belongs among the texts of the period which our own modernity has not yet been able to confront, perhaps because the Schillerian aesthetic categories, whether we know it or not, are still the taken-for-granted premises of our own pedagogical, historical and political ideologies" ("Aesthetic Formalization in Kleist," 266).

The review takes for granted the rhetoric and the ideology of the symbol, with its values of continuity, organicity, homogeneity, symmetry, and totality, and, in a gesture akin to Husserl's use of the term "European" in his defensive demarcation of the properly philosophical, maps them onto European culture based on a rigid logic of national stereotyping. As Hamacher comments, "It can appear as a logic, as a consistent mode of thought, because it makes the claim that the nation, the national community, is itself a homogeneous and substantial form not only of that which has been thought, but of thought itself. Therefore nationalism is a substantialism—a substantialism of community conceived of as nature" ("Journals, Politics," 439). Gasché and Chase, among others, point out that the ideo-logic of nationalism in the wartime writings does not simply serve the interests of the occupying power: "The issue which is a decisive thread running through most of the articles—the concern with national personality and difference, patriotic feeling, the protection . . . of national patrimony, the persistence of the independence of nationalities—is incongruous with the dominant Nazi ideology" (Gasché, "Edges of Understanding," 211). "The presence in the articles of such stereotyping by no means amounts to celebration of German nationality or the German nation; the characteristic qualities of at least three nations, France, Belgium, and Germany, are being identified and valued, in terms exerting some check or pressure upon the design of German domination. But while the stereotyping thus lacks a direct and pro-Nazi political significance, its deeper ideological significance persists" (Chase, "Trappings," 50). Symptomatic of that ideological significance, as Chase remarks, is the fact that the young de Man's "strongest interest or enthusiasm is elicited by the co-presence of these [national] qualities or the circumvention of their opposition" (50), which he finds, for example, in Goethe's novel: "a latin as well as a germanic sensibility will be touched by its content in every sense. . . . one could take pains to situate the *Elective Affinities* in the norm of the literary traditions of all the great European creative centres. We will limit ourselves to examining the work with respect to the French and German artistic qualities: the synthesis of these two national temperaments, a rare and uneasy realization, being already amply sufficient to justify its particular attraction" (de Man, "Universalisme de Goethe," 238). The balance of the review is given over to this examination, culminating in the final paragraph: "In conclusion, this conjunction, in the same work, of so many different qualities, a conjunction obtained without the unity of the narrative and of the thought suffering for an instant, confers on it an unequaled merit. . . . At certain moments, the totality of riches dispersed among the nations forming western civilization are concentrated in an elect, who thus becomes the universal genius. With this work, we witness one of these unique moments in the history of letters" (239).

Such claims help to specify the blindness that crippled de Man's understanding in much of the wartime journalism. In a review of A. E. Brinckmann's *Geist der Nationen* (which he also cotranslated), he writes that "What is proper to our time is the consideration of this national personality as a valuable condition, as a precious possession, which has to be maintained at the cost of all sacrifices. This conception is miles apart from sentimental patriotism. Rather, it concerns a sober faith, a practical means to defend Western culture against a decomposition from the inside or an overwhelming onrush by neighboring cultural norms" (de Man, "Culture and Art," 303; originally published in *Het Vlaamsche Land* on March 29–30, 1942). Weber discerns the "pattern of self-mystification that accompanies the experience of crisis" here, commenting that

> What is 'proper to our time,' then, is not simply the valorization of the national or of nationalism, but rather the sense of these values being threatened: by internal 'decomposition' or by 'surprise attack.' What is 'proper to our time,' in short, is the sense of danger from without and from within. . . . It is not enough to define the identity of Europe internally, as it were, in terms of the 'mutual exchanges' of the different national groups that inhabit the European continent. That identity must also be *set off* and *apart from* what it is not, from the non-European, the foreign. That is, from the Other. . . . Totality is never whole. . . . The other of the European . . . is, first and foremost: the Jew. It is the Jews who intrude, deranging the 'continuity' and immanence of Western History: in this case, that of German Literature, thus causing it to deviate from its proper, predestined course. ("Monument Disfigured," 416)

The rhetoric of crisis is here yoked to the logic of nationalism as agonism that may be understood to yield (or, minimally, not to prevent) arguments such as those in de Man's article "The Jews in Contemporary Literature,"[11] also published in *Le Soir*. Thus the ideologue's "stereotypes, along with the models of thought they propagate, become among the most appalling products of the century" (Hamacher, "Journals, Politics," 438).

As tactically deployed and maneuvered in de Man's review of the translation of *The Elective Affinities*, the national stereotypes operate for the most part along predictable ideological lines. The traits that align the novel with "the great French classical tradition" also account for its strikingly "modern accent," chief among them "the eternal leitmotif of French prose: the primacy of the psychological motive." "In no recent work, even in an age in which the knowledge of the human soul has made considerable progress and the psychological *tournure d'esprit* has become more commonplace, can one indicate a clearer, more coherent analysis. The perfect harmony between the introspective and active parts of the content, the fact that each gesture finds its equivalent in the profound conformation of the one who performs it, these are the fundamental virtues that we find here" ("Universalisme de Goethe," 238). The "'French' virtues" of the novel, then, are those of "the equilibrium and mutual rapport of the component parts," the "perfection of the proportions among the different elements," "the rigor of the logical arrangement"—or, as he enumerates in "Le problème français. *Dieu est-il français?* de F. Sieburg," "the virtues of clarity, logic, harmony" that comprise "the constants of the latin spirit" (de Man, "Le problème français," 226–27; originally published in *Le Soir* on April 28, 1942).

Other aspects of Goethe's text, however, serve to remind the reader that it is "contemporaneous with that flowering of the germanic genius that is German Romanticism." De Man's review maintains that key elements in the novel exceed the psychological and the rational ("not everything is clarified by simple reason"), indicating a "supernatural power that eludes all analysis." "The death of the two lovers," for example "which is not explained by any illness or any physiological fact, symbolizes a supra-terrestrial union, and thus no longer belongs to the realm of tangible verisimilitude." He remarks "the violence of certain passions that are raised above all contingency to enter into eternity," assimilating it to "the metaphysical sentiment of the infinite proper to German thought," through which "the novel reflects the nationality of its author" ("Universalisme de Goethe," 239). (Given that he is writing about a French translation of Goethe's prose, it is worth noting the absence here of anything presaging the mature reflection on translation, on the constitutive distance dividing the translated text from the original, that de Man provides in his late lecture on Walter Benjamin's "The Task of the Translator," entitled "Conclusions" and collected in *The Resistance to Theory*.)

Finally, he aligns *The Elective Affinities* with the German literary tradition by way of its subordination of aesthetic to ethical interests: If in the French canon "from Racine to Gide" moral dilemmas are posed only for the sake of their aesthetic potential, "it is completely otherwise in the present case": Goethe's "profound germanism" enlists the aesthetic in the service of the ethical, "drawing practical conclusions with respect to education and to conduct" ("Universalisme de Goethe," 239). The same set of priorities is associated with the German tradition throughout the wartime journalism—for example, in a review of Paul Willems's "Tout est réel ici" (published in *Le Soir* on July 15, 1941), in "Le problème français. *Dieu est-il français?* de F. Sieburg" (published in *Le Soir* on April 28, 1942), and in "People and Books. A View on Contemporary German Fiction" (published in *Het Vlaamsche Land* on August 20, 1942), where de Man observes that "in present-day Germany there lives and flourishes a literature which is directly connected with that of the great precursors," with "the profound essence of [Germany's] artistic genius," "the spiritual property of the nation." The leitmotif (the red thread, as Goethe famously figures it) accounting for this continuity is "the profound moral disposition . . . the ambitious treatment of ethical problems," "the proper traditions of German art which had always and before everything else clung to a deep spiritual sincerity." That tradition, he argues here, was challenged in postwar German culture by the expressionist movement, in the work of "non-Germans, and specifically Jews," who pursued "an art with a strongly cerebral disposition, founded upon some abstract principles and very remote from all naturalness," resulting in "skillful artifices aimed at easy effects," and "a forced, caricatured representation of reality" ("People and Books," 325).

Gasché's nuanced analysis of this blinded "View" points out among other things that "the cerebral quality of expressionism, that sets it over and against the other type of German literature, is an attribute associated throughout all the articles not only with Jewish thinking"—as in the reference to the Jews' "strongly cerebral disposition" in "The Jews in Contemporary Literature"—"but with French culture in particular" (Gasché, "Edges of Understanding," 210; cf. de Man's "cérébralité qui a triomphé dans les lettres françaises de l'époque actuelle," "Le destin de la Flandre," 139). This cerebrality, abstraction, and artifice are among the traits he will ascribe, in "The Rhetoric of Temporality," to allegory. Indeed, de Man's late work itself "exhibits all the negative characteristics cited by the young Paul: cerebrality, abstraction, a tendency to 'différencier à outrance'" (Johnson, "Preface to the Paperback Edition," xvi). But in the wartime journalism, the values associated with the symbol prevail virtually unchallenged.

Those values give the impetus to articles such as "Le destin de la Flandre" (139–40; originally published in *Le Soir* on September 1, 1941), a programmatic text in which de Man seeks to define and demarcate "the nation" (in this instance, the Flemish nation), to establish its origin and its essence according to aesthetic criteria. The particular "genius" of Flemish art, with its "elective virtues" of pictorialism and realism, accords Flanders the status of an art-nation whose cultural and political autonomy must be preserved in the face of the current imperialist threat ("one can pose the question of its political destiny only as a function of its cultural qualities") ("Le destin de la Flandre," 139, 140). Hamacher assesses the ideological import of this national aestheticism:

> as a theory of the originality, autonomy and essence of a nation, [it] demonstrates unmistakable affinities with the national-aesthetic myths of origin propagated in fascist Germany at the same time. There can be no doubt about the proto-fascist substance of this theory. But—with it de Man makes himself the defender of the art-nation Flanders against the cultural and political imperialisms of the neighboring nations and above all against the pan-Germanic annexation policy of the National Socialist regime. De Man turns the national-aesthetic ideologeme—which not only suited the occupation powers and their organized Belgian supporters, but was even borrowed from their own ideological resources—against the Nazi's integration plans . . . and uses it as an argument not only for the cultural autonomy but also for the political independence of Belgium. ("Journals, Politics," 443)[12]

A few months later, in a review of Willems's "Tout est réel ici," de Man argues the participation of Belgian fantastic realism, the outgrowth of Flemish pictorial realism, in both the German romantic and the French surrealist traditions, at no cost to its (relative) autonomy. In this sense, contemporary Belgian art is the privileged locus of the synthesis of the great cultural blocs of Europe, France, and Germany, now at war. "But what in the antagonistic art-nations ought to join together to create this Belgian unity must itself already have the character of the European synthesis": it is in this context that "de Man praises Goethe's combination of a *sensibilité latine* and a *sensibilité germanique, la sythèse de ces deux tempéra-*

ments nationaux; and he lauds Ernst Jünger, the only other German author for whom he shows unrestrained admiration, for his combination of myth and reality" (Hamacher, "Journals, Politics," 454).

Given the virtually uninterrupted, rapid-fire deployment of national stereotypes in these articles, those few junctures at which the reviewer hesitates, however briefly, may warrant further consideration. In the course of enumerating the "'French' virtues" of Goethe's novel ("the rare perfection of the proportions . . . the rigor of the logical arrangements," etc.), de Man writes that "One point in this admirable architecture"—one of the novel's own figures for proportion, balance, and symmetry—"merits that one pause over it longer." This is followed by the sentences, singled out by Hamacher as written by a reader rather than an ideologue, on the "strange interlude" early in the novel's second part, which suspends the narrative development, but functions crucially to introduce "the factor of time, of the *duration* of events" ("Universalisme de Goethe," 238). De Man pauses, takes time (a quantity in short supply in journalism, particularly of the daily variety) to single out for attention the place where the novel itself pauses, interrupts itself to introduce the time factor. He takes the time, that is—if only a moment—to read. The review then resumes its prescribed ideological course, and its brisk pace, as de Man goes on to align the introduction of the time factor, of duration, with "the 'French' virtues of the 'Affinities,'" ascribing it to the "rigor of the logical arrangement," specifically that of the mimetic logic of realism: "a narrative which aims to produce the real rhythm of existence must insert such epochs" ("Universalisme de Goethe," 238). He then proceeds directly to catalogue the novel's "German" features.

To read such a passage now, after the fact (or facts: the fact of its first and its second appearance, the fact of the late work), is in part to ask whether "the factor of time" can indeed be understood as contingent (upon national origin, for example), whether it can be subsumed under one or another "logical arrangement." The de Man of "The Rhetoric of Temporality" and the essays that followed would answer that, where texts are concerned, it cannot. When the factor of time is understood not as contingent but as constitutive, it resists assimilation to such a logic (of nationalism, of realism, of blindness and insight). In the review of *The Elective Affinities*, it may serve to skew the opposition and the synthesis of the art-nations, as allegory skews the symbol, as the fact that the foundation stone of the summerhouse is also and at the same time [*zugleich*] a memorial stone—at once a time capsule and a grave marker—may skew the spatial symmetry of the "admirable architecture" of the building and of the novel itself.

The "introduction of the time factor," then, may be understood to disrupt the rhetoric and the ideology of the symbol that, when mapped onto European culture and politics in 1940–43, yielded the national aestheticism (the phrase is Philippe Lacoue-Labarthe's, in his *La fiction du politique*) that determines much of the wartime journalism. The argument of de Man's late work, its theoretical reflection on rhetoric and ideology, is that, in Hartman's succinct paraphrase, "Any mode of analysis that sees the text as an organicist unity or uses it for a totalizing purpose is blind, and the text itself will 'deconstruct' such disclosures" ("Looking Back," 19). This would include the argument of his unpublished lecture on *The Elective Affinities*.

The lecture begins by invoking the novel's "sombre," "upsetting," and "haunting" qualities, suggesting that the reader "can be unaware of [the] sombreness until it catches hold" with a "belated shock effect" (like that of a time bomb). De Man goes on to assert that the novel's "dreamlike" overdeterminations are "not symbolic, not transposable into a single symbolic register," that the "different registers [are] not necessarily compatible." The claims that he makes for the unity of the novel's symbolic system in the *Le Soir* review are in the late lecture subsumed under the first of "three levels of reading." The initial level or moment is that of "trope," of the text's "literal [and] figural diction."[13] "This novel is, more than any other text you can read, about language," and de Man's reading first takes into account its system of symmetrical "exchanges" and "substitutions." He offers a "summary in terms of geometrical figures" of the relations among the principal characters: They are "structured like a circle or rather a sphere," and also as a "cross";

the tropology thus draws on the "highly formalized, symbolic language" of Rosicrucianism and freemasonry that "hangs over eighteenth and nineteenth century literature." He mentions *Wilhelm Meister* and *Die Zauberflöte* and adds, ironically, "once you're aware of this you'll go crazy. The less you know about it the better." That irony takes a sharp turn in light of the wartime journalism, for example, de Man's "Introduction to Contemporary German Literature" (200–1; originally published in *Le Soir* on March 2, 1942), an account of the 1942 German Book Exposition that Alice Yaeger Kaplan calls the "rhetorical apogee of de Man's collaborative writing" ("Paul de Man," 276).[14] The cross within the circle figures the "principle of totalization" conveyed most notably through the "analogy of the chemical reactions" elaborated in the novel's fourth chapter. In the "equation between elements" ($CaCO_3 + SO_4H_2 = CaSO_4 + CO_2 + H_2O$), the "original formulation is symmetrical," reflecting the "balance," the "specular relation between [the] two sides of [the] equal sign" and "allowing for crossing over." The "affinities [that] develop" between Eduard and Ottilie, the Captain and Charlotte do so according to this "rigorously symmetrical" model, hence the "double adultery," the "double resemblance" in the child, the "baptism [of the child]" and the "death [of the priest]." That "symmetry is the principle of totalization" that organizes the narrative.

It is fitting that the chemical formula provided is that for limestone and gypsum, for the "principle of building" that is a "constant" in the novel "is itself a principle of symmetry." Its thematic function is multiple, since building (e.g., the construction of the summerhouse) is also "the figure of marriage," "tied to the institution of marriage" as a "balance between *Blutverwandtschaft* (filiation) and *Seelenverwandtschaft* (affinity)," between the genetic and the erotic (he here alludes to Walter Benjamin's essay on the novel and its citation of Kant's *Metaphysics of Morals*, which defines marriage as "the union of two people of different sexes in lifelong reciprocal possession of one another's sexual properties"). Thus the "equation sets [the] pattern of the book. [The] polarities, by crossing over, result in totalizations," "all under [the] aegis of [the] fundamental metaphor of building," of "*Stiftung* as the grounding of an institution," the "property on which the stability of [the] balance [between] genetic [and] erotic rests." And the story itself, "based on [the] principle of symmetry," is as such "like a building, an architectonic."

De Man here reads the text's symmetries in terms of the tropological function of language, the operation of figures such as metaphor and chiasmus: The "elaborate system of symmetries," of "specular relations," is "one of [the] powerful forces of trope—it is the system of trope, [with] its overdeterminations," that establishes the "integrated unity in [the] presentation of the novel" ("everything relates to everything else") that the young journalist praised in the *Le Soir* review. But in the lecture, de Man goes on to discern a "disturbance of [the] symmetry on the level of tropes." And it is here that the later encounter with *The Elective Affinities* locates the intervention of the time factor, for this disturbance occurs "temporally": "what seems to work in space doesn't work on [the] temporal level." As evidence, he cites the insistent role in the narrative of "impatience" and "haste" [*Eile*], associated especially with the impetuous Eduard, who "plays the flute too hurriedly" in his duets with Charlotte, such that the "tempos don't coincide." He recalls as well the symptomatic scene of reading in which "Charlotte runs ahead in reading over [his] shoulder as Eduard reads aloud," resulting in a "distortion that disrupts [the] spontaneous illusion of representation, of voice, in reading"; Eduard likens the effect to being "torn in two," a figure that anticipates the subsequent fate of Nanni, Ottilie's companion, who is "literally" dismembered (then re-membered) near the novel's end. Such "confusion of literal and figurative" accounts for the always possible "fundamental error of reading, of interpretation" that consists in "taking one for the other"—as in taking death for life in the *tableau vivant*, which depends on effects "achieved by trope" for its "complex balance of life and death." "To represent dead painting as alive is [a] mistake. The *tableau* is not *vivant*"—with consequences for Goethe's text, whose "narration in [the] present [tense]" affords a "succession of *tableaux vivants*." The sense that "reading is dangerous in the novel" is confirmed when, in the "movement from adultery to infanticide" in the narrative's "succession of crimes," the drowning of the child is presented "as a result of Ottilie's reading" (in a scene in which she is represented allegorically, as the "emblematic figure of the patron saint of Alsace, book in hand," fatally forgetful of death). The "system of symmetrical tropes is undone in this play with life and death." More precisely, the symmetry established "at the level of trope [is] undone by temporality," "disturbed by a temporal lack of convergence," by the introduction of the factor of time. "The epistemological asymmetry of knowing" is a *temporal* asymmetry: "things don't come together in time." Yet this "undoing" can be "recuperated on [the] level of representation," to the extent that this story of negative knowledge can still be told.

The lecture goes on to elaborate what disrupts or resists totalization in terms of other moments of reading, other functions of language. De Man invokes the "level" or "system of the letter," the "asemantic" function associated with the terms *Buchstabe* ("mistranslated as symbol") and *Zeichensprache*, and embodied in the figure of Ottilie as "allegorically overdetermined element" (the several characters "thematize" one or another "linguistic function": "there are no persons in this book"). In scenes such as that in which Ottilie copies Eduard's contract ("by means of which property is acquired, [the] house set up") in handwriting that comes to resemble his own—or in which, at any rate, he can only see his own—the "crossing takes place on the literal level of *Handschrift*," of the "materiality of writing, of inscription." The "level of the letter" "undoes [the] level of representation, of trope"; it is "no longer [a] thematics, no longer [the] realm of trope and substitution," "no longer of [the] order of representation," but rather of the order of "allegory." The fate of the characters is "inscribed in the nature of language": "Ottilie becomes mute, [the] letter loses its voice." And the "hopelessness of this is intolerable. Hard to take. No escape. Intolerable. That's the way it is."

Finally, de Man suggests the possibility of a further "recuperation" at the "level of narrative control" (of "Goethe's 'wir'"), a possibility he terms "dialogism."[15] But again, the intervention of time renders this recovery incomplete. For in the novel itself, "wrong stories [are] constantly being told at [the] wrong time," in the manner of "gaffes" that are "fine, coherent as stories, but told in untimely fashion," with results that are "deeply and fundamentally embarrassing," indeed "catastrophic" (he recalls the effects of Mittler's remarks on Ottilie, and especially those of the interpolated tale of the "strange young neighbors" on Charlotte). For readers of the novel, the lecture concludes, the dialogic "asymmetry" raises the questions: "is [Goethe's] story timely for us? Can we attain Goethe's serenity?" The answer afforded in the lecture—a far cry from the reassuring assertion of the "universalism of Goethe" in the early review—is that the story "never comes at the right time," is "always untimely," that it is "always a catastrophe to understand it." "This is dialogism—[the] fundamental asymmetry of [the] dialogical situation": the asymmetry between the text and its reading that troubles our own efforts to read the past in the present, to read (for example) the wartime journalism in this, its second phase of use.

If we reread the *Le Soir* review of *The Elective Affinities* in the retrospective light of the late lecture, we find that the apparent unity, symmetry, and harmony that the former prizes in Goethe's novel are made possible by a highly formalized system of tropes, a system on which knowledge and cognition depend. The moment in which the review pauses to consider the time factor—and so, potentially, its disfiguring, asymmetricalizing effect, its exposure of the precarious status of the text's totalizations—is immediately reinscribed in the symbolic system according to the mechanism analyzed in de Man's late work whereby the threat posed to cognition is, inevitably but erroneously, reinscribed in a tropological system, whereby the historical event is recuperated for, implemented in, one or another aesthetic and political program. It would be left to essays like "Aesthetic Formalization in Kleist" to analyze "the complicity between the aesthetic valorization of form"—specifically the model of trope, the "transformational turns and substitutive exchanges of which are necessarily informed by a telos of infinite totalization"—and "totalitarian claims to hegemony" (Weber, "Monument Disfigured," 413, 415). The late essays seek to elaborate, to make explicit the articulation of "textual models and the historical and political systems that are their correlate" (de Man, "Aesthetic Formalization in Kleist," 289). As Chase suggests, "the correlation . . . between a totalitarian state and a model of the text as a 'formal system of tropes' (*The Rhetoric of Romanticism*, 285) is more than an impression and other than an analogy" ("Trappings," 55). The burden imposed by the correlation of the textual and the political, like that imposed by the attempt to articulate early with late de Man, is that of reading: The relations (whether of continuity and complicity, or discontinuity and distance) cannot be presumed, but must be read, again and again, in each here and now. "The suspension of the necessity of reading needs to be resisted because it closes down the possibility of a future. In doing so, it is inevitably totalitarian, whereas reading, in suspending, is not *inevitably* totalitarian, which does not mean that it is inevitably democratic either—reading is not inevitably anything, that's why it holds out the promise of a future" (Warminski, "Terrible Reading," 387–88).

This is also the burden (and the promise) of the effort to correlate text and history, the order of language and the order of the event. It is the burden assumed, in no uncertain terms, in de Man's late work. As Weber argues, the conception of history in the essays from "Shelley Disfigured" to "Kant and Schiller" is entirely distinct from that advanced in the articles published in *Le Soir* and *Het Vlaamsche Land*, for example in "Criticism and Literary History," where history appears as a "continuity" in which "one generation ensues logically from the preceding one" (313–14; originally published in *Het Vlaamsche Land* on June 7–8, 1942); the two understandings "are separated by a practice of reading which is both informed by a theory of language and which transforms it in turn" (Weber, "Monument Disfigured," 413–14). The order of events, as theorized in de Man's mature writings, is assimilable neither to a logic (or dialectics) nor to the tropology of cognition, nor, finally, to temporality. History, as "Kant and Schiller" demonstrates, is not a movement of mediation, not a temporal process, but a radical transformation "from cognition, from acts of knowledge, from states of cognition, to something which is no longer a cognition but which is to some extent an *occurrence*, which has the materiality of something that actually happens, that actually occurs . . . that leaves a trace on the world" (de Man, "Kant and Schiller," 132). In this sense, history is "*what is happening*," as Derrida writes, and "happening to *us*" (Derrida, "Like the Sound," 128). For Derrida, as for de Man, as for Goethe's eloquent mason, history "belongs to the order of the absolutely unforeseeable, which is always the condition of any event"—for example, the disclosure of the wartime journalism. "Even when it seems to go back to a buried past, what comes about always comes from the future" (Derrida, "Like the Sound," 128): from the work to come.

PART TWO

In the wake of television

§ 3 No time like the present

HISTORY: Anything that appears on television.

—Lewis H. Lapham, "Economic Correctness"[1]

Where will you be the next time history happens?

—CNN self-advertisement, 1996 and early 1997

As a point of departure, let me recall a passage from a recent essay entitled "Journals, Politics":

> Many years ago—it might already be twenty—Max Horkheimer recommended a little experiment during a television interview. He suggested reading newspapers a few weeks or months after their publication. With this he bent over to pick up a stack of rather gray papers that lay next to his chair.
>
> I cannot recall his comments on this piece of advice. But one can imagine that the effect he had in mind was supposed to be both philosophical and political. Indeed, *the effect of this small postponement on the reader, on his perception of time and on his attitude to news and published opinion, should be considerable.* The reader of these old papers will notice that the imperatives, attractions and threats heralded in them reveal themselves *as* such only to the degree that they no longer directly affect him. The judgments that the newspapers imposed on him at another time can now be dismissed as hectic presumptions. In the future he will no longer so easily obey the regulations of the newspapers and their time. . . . Horkheimer's is a piece of political advice that looks forward to the suspension of coercion and to its transformation for another way of life. (Hamacher, "Journals, Politics," 457, some emphasis added)

It is telling that this philosophically and politically instructive mise-en-scène took place "during a television interview" in the frame afforded by what Paul Virilio has termed the "third window." And it may be worth asking what such an experiment might yield when brought to bear *on* television, as a medium with its own specificity.

A still-suggestive locus for reflection on what distinguishes television from other media is the formulation provided by Stephen Heath and Gillian Skirrow in their pivotal essay "Television: A World in Action": "What is specific to television—the possibility of 'live broadcasting,' the present electronic production of the image—becomes the term of its exploited imaginary, the generalized fantasy . . . that is, that the image is direct, and direct for me . . . which fantasy is then taken for the ground reality of television and its programs."[2] What still recommends this analysis, which (like Horkheimer's scenario) is by now more than twenty years old, is the remarkable economy with which it designates two crucial components of the televisual imaginary that have come to be generalized—that is, to be taken as the basis for a *theory* of television as medium, theory being the grounding of the interpretation and evaluation of the object in a general conceptual system. Those components are first, the fantasy that the image is *direct* (i.e., that it functions as if it were not produced, by way of a particular technics or technology of *re*presentation, but were somehow an unmediated, straightforward presentation); and second, the concomitant fantasy that the image is *direct for me* (as if it were unproblematically addressed to me, presented to me, in a here and now that I share with the imaged event).

In categorical terms, at stake here are fundamental presuppositions about the relation between the order of perception and the order of cognition, including the assumption that, especially where so-called "live" broadcasting is concerned, visibility translates as cognitive availability. Following Heath and Skirrow, Jane Feuer has elaborated a critique of the mechanism whereby the presumed ontology of television, defined in accordance with the possibility of the instantaneous recording, broadcasting, and reception of the event, becomes (once again) generalized as a theory of television. Accompanying that generalization (and recall that what is generalized is a fantasy, a highly seductive one) is an ideologization that it becomes crucial, for philosophical as well as political reasons, to resist. Such resistance begins with recalling the medium in its difference not only from other media, but from itself.[3]

When we forget the differential specificity of broadcast television in particular, what we forget, first and foremost, is time. As Mary Ann Doane argues persuasively in her essay "Information, Crisis, Catastrophe," "Time is television's basis, its principle of structuration as well as its persistent reference. The insistence of the temporal attribute may indeed be a characteristic of all systems of imaging enabled by mechanical or electronic reproduction" (222).[4] An anecdotal instance may serve to bring this home, affording a reminder of what we are too liable to forget (and constituting, in effect, my own inadvertent experiment). Several seasons back, I was working on a preliminary version of what eventually would become this text as the Senate Judiciary Committee's hearings on the confirmation of Clarence Thomas as Supreme Court justice—what ABC correspondent Jack Smith characterized at the time as "perhaps the most riveting television since Watergate or the McCarthy hearings"—were broadcast "live" by the American networks (including CNN, which became a full partner with ABC, CBS, and NBC during its saturation "coverage" of the war in the Persian Gulf earlier in the same year[5]). For the most part, I listened to the hearings on National Public Radio, with the TV on but the sound muted. At a certain point on the afternoon of October 12, 1991, I looked up from my draft and over at the other screen and saw that the video image of the hearings bore a caption whose variants are familiar to viewers of broadcast news: "NBC, Live 5:00 EDT." I then discerned that the video and audio were out of synch, that the radio transmission emerged in advance of the sound restored to the televised image that was nonetheless emphatically labeled "live."

To return to the terms provided by Hamacher in "Journals, Politics": The "effect of this small postponement"—not a matter of a few weeks or months, as in Horkheimer's proposed experiment with print journalism, but of less than a second—the effect on my perception of time and on my attitude toward what I was seeing and hearing was indeed "considerable" (457). The successive judgments imposed by the broadcast became recognizable, however fleetingly, as the hectic presumptions they were. Or rather, the crucial difference between judgment and presumption itself became readable, thinkable. Not by chance, the context was the unfolding of a drama, and specifically a trial scene, one that persisted in invoking the "truth" ("Only one of them is telling the truth," intoned senators and commentators alike; "What really happened between Anita Hill and Clarence Thomas?") but that was, *as* trial scene, a sustained exercise in persuasion, a deployment of rhetoric for political interests and ends, and not for the sake of establishing the truth or the meaning of past and present events. (This is not to suggest, with some of the right-wing members of the committee and the media, as well as Thomas himself, that Hill was the tool or the dupe of interest groups; the assumption that she was indeed "telling the truth" about "what really happened" does not change the rhetorical status of the scene itself.)

Predictably enough, the video images of the hearings were promptly noted, sorted, and glossed in print. As a television critic for the *Los Angeles Times* observed, "Some of the pictures have conveyed self-contained dramas in themselves," among them the spectacle of "Senators on both sides quoting newspapers as automatic truth when it was in their best interests, then attacking newspapers when it wasn't" (Rosenberg, "High Noon," F10). We confront, then, the typically vicious circle in which newspapers quote TV quoting newspapers—and whatever sense we can make of this will depend on the truth value accorded to these media in the first place.

This returns us to what Doane, in the context of an analysis of disinformation as an abuse of broadcast television, calls the "automatic truth value associated with this mode of dissemination" ("Information, Crisis, Catastrophe," 224), a truth value that is predicated in large part on our investments in so-called "live" television, generalized as a model and which is "then taken for the ground reality of television and its programs" (Heath and Skirrow, "Television").

(Another indication of this "automatic truth value" was an item reported as part of the media response to Oliver Stone's controversial film *JFK*. A poll taken many years after the Kennedy assassination disclosed that an overwhelming number of Americans—at least as many as believe the Dallas events were part of a conspiracy—were convinced that they had seen the assassination live on television, though the Zapruder film languished in a vault at Time-Life until five years later and was only made available as still photographs in the interim. In this case, the "effect of [the] postponement" was again "considerable": It involved the belated substitution of the mediated image for the then and there of an event supremely associated with the occlusion of truth, its failure to come to light.[6]

The unproblematic articulation of live TV with the real (and with real time) has its impulse in a broader realist ideology that finds its opportunity in the failure to reflect on the medium, on the distances of space and time that characterize its structure and effects.[7] A telling instance of this forgetting occurs in an essay by Stanley Cavell, symptomatically entitled "The Fact of Television," in which he posits "the material basis of television as *a current of simultaneous event reception*. This," he writes, "is how I am conceiving of the aesthetic fact of television that I propose to begin portraying" (252). Cavell's analysis treads the path marked out by his earlier attempts, in *The World Viewed*, "to distinguish the fact of movies from the fact of theater, on the blatant ground that in a theater the actors appear in person and in a film they do not" ("Fact of Television," 251). He recalls André Bazin's argument in *What is Cinema?* that film "relays the actors' presence to us as by mirrors" (Bazin, *What is Cinema?*, 97). Cavell is then struck, after the "fact," that "Bazin's idea here really fits the fact of live television, in which what we are presented with is happening *simultaneously* with its presentation. This," he concludes, "remains reasonably blatant, anyway unsurprising" (Cavell, "Fact of Television," 252). What is perhaps surprising is Cavell's obliviousness to the temporal complications not only of the medium, but of his own argumentation, which operates in large part by citing his own past formulations, preserving their syntax as he substitutes fresh terms supposed to correspond to the televisual instance.

The characterization of "the material basis of television," the "aesthetic fact of television," as "*a current of simultaneous event reception*" thus unfolds over against Cavell's former "provisional, summary characterization of the material basis of movies, apart from which there would be nothing to call a movie. . . . I call the basis *a succession of automatic world projections*" ("Fact of Television," 251, citing *World Viewed*, 72). The multiple substitutions involved here ("current" and "simultaneous" for "succession" and "automatic," "event" for "world," "reception" for "projections") ground a further distinction: "The mode of perception that I claim is called upon by film's material basis is what I call viewing. The mode of perception I wish to think about in connection with television's material basis is that of *monitoring*" ("Fact of Television," 252), which is to say "preparing our attention to be called upon by certain eventualities"—monitoring "as in monitoring the heart, or the rapid eye movements during periods of dreaming—say, monitoring signs of life" (258). For, as he takes the occasion to affirm, "where there's life, there's hope" (254). He goes on to admit (hopefully?) that his definition of television's material basis leaves out transmission and broadcasting as integral to television's operation and hence leaves out of account the difficulties that these crucial functions would pose for his model and his argument.[8]

Cavell observes further of "the amount of talk that runs across" television's formats that "the frequent description of television as providing 'company' . . . is [partly] a function of the simultaneity of the medium—or of *the fact that at any time it might be live* and that there is no sensuous distinction between the live and the repeat, or the replay: the others are *there*, if not shut in this room, still caught at this time. One is receiving them or monitoring them, like callers; and receiving or monitoring, unlike screening and projection, does not come between their presence to the camera and their presentness to us" ("Fact of Television," 253, some emphasis added). But if the medium's temporality is not, cannot be, one of precise simultaneity, something does come between, and we find ourselves in the more disconcerting "company" of ghosts. Strictly speaking, television is *never* live: for, as Jacques Derrida once observed in a videotaped interview, "When the very *first* perception of an image is linked to a structure of reproduction, then we are dealing with the realm of phantoms" (Payne and Lewis, "Ghost Dance," 61).

Although Cavell's stated aim is to establish the "aesthetic *fact* of television," his essay clearly puts forward a *theory* of the medium, based once again on a generalization of "live" broadcasting. The confusion of fact and theory (we are not here in the realm invoked by Walter Benjamin, citing Goethe, where "all factuality is already theory" [Letter to Martin Buber, 132]), as well as the collapse of the distinction between the "aesthetic fact" and the "material basis," are themselves effects of what Paul de Man has termed "aesthetic ideology." In this context, de Man's analysis has much to contribute to the possibility of reading the differential specificity of television.

As the preceding chapter recalls, that analysis entails a sustained investigation of the values associated, at least since the eighteenth century, with symbolical and allegorical conceptions of language. In "The Rhetoric of Temporality," de Man interrogates the way in which "the supremacy of the symbol, conceived as an expression of unity between the representative and the semantic functions of language, becomes [in the nineteenth century] a commonplace that underlies literary taste, literary criticism, and literary history," as well as the extent to which the symbol "still functions as the basis of recent French and English studies of the romantic and postromantic eras" (189–90). He argues that the symbol, a figure predicated on the presumed continuity and simultaneity of "the sensory image and the supersensory totality that the image suggests," in turn grounds an understanding of the subject–object relation "in which the experience of the object takes on the form of a perception or a sensation. The ultimate intent of the image is synthesis," he writes, and "the mode of this synthesis is defined as symbolic by the priority conferred on the initial moment of sensory perception"—that is, on the *aesthetic* moment (193). The symbol, then, proves to be the linguistic condition of possibility of a certain claim for the autonomy and the power of the aesthetic.

De Man's analysis demonstrates that the symbol, rather than

serving as the legitimate basis for a theory of language as such, is "a special case of figural language in general, a special case that can lay no claim to historical or philosophical priority over other figures," including allegory ("Rhetoric of Temporality," 191). Allegory disrupts the possibility of the symbolic synthesis by opening up a constitutive temporal dimension, the difference that divides the allegorical sign from the previous sign to which it refers: "The meaning constituted by the allegorical sign can then consist only in the *repetition* . . . of a previous sign with which it can never coincide, since it is of the essence of this previous sign to be pure anteriority. Whereas the symbol postulates the possibility of an identity or identification, allegory designates primarily a distance in relation to its own origin, and, renouncing the nostalgia and the desire to coincide, it establishes its language in the void of this temporal difference" (207). Allegory confesses the failure of coincidence forgotten or repressed in the symbol, in which the relationship of representation and substance, image and event, is taken to be "one of simultaneity, which, in truth, is spatial in kind, and in which the intervention of time is merely a matter of contingency" (207).

De Man's argument effects a radical revision of conventional literary-historical and aesthetic categories, disrupting the rhetoric and the ideology of the symbol, with its values of continuity, organicity, homogeneity, symmetry, and totality. If we read his analysis of aesthetic ideology into one recent lament for the decline of print and the ascendancy of electronic media, we may at least adumbrate its potential for coming to terms with television. Alvin Kernan, in his essay "The Death of Literature," which summarizes the thesis of his book of the same title, warns that "in an age in which television, not books, will define the realm of knowledge, the concept of literature could easily disappear. Television is not symbiotic with literature the way that print was. Literary values—authors, great works, deep meanings—fitted hand-in-glove with print, but television both weakens literacy (the skill on which literature depends) and undercuts literature's basic functions. The replacement of the printed word by the image and the voice substitutes immediate, powerful one-dimensional pictures and simple continuities for the ironies, ambiguities, and complex structures fostered by print and idealized in literature"[9] ("Death of Literature," 11). For Kernan, then, aesthetic values are not only compatible with the complex linguistic structures "fostered by print and idealized by literature" (a compatibility that de Man calls into serious question)—their relation is continuous, "symbiotic," "hand-in-glove." Hence his claim, his point of departure and point of return, that romantic and modern literature's "leading values were aesthetic versions of print logic" ("Death of Literature," 11).

Cavell's own starting point is "an effort to get at something one can see as the aesthetic interest of television. That there is such an interest invited by, related to, but different from, an interest in what we call its economy, its sociology, and its psychology, and that this interest is still insufficiently understood—which contributes to an insufficiently developed critical tradition concerning television . . . is the point from which any contribution I may make to it is apt to proceed" (Cavell, "Fact of Television," 250–51). Although Cavell's judgment that television has thus far eluded sustained theoretical scrutiny may be valid, his own "contribution" is arguably a setback rather than an advance for a reading of the medium.[10] For what he specifies as the "aesthetic fact of television"—a current of simultaneous event reception—marks the point of convergence between aesthetic ideology and an ideology of realism that "finds the final guarantee of reality in the power of so-called *facts*. This reality," as Hamacher rightly insists, "is actually first generated by all sorts of societal—and not only societal—institutions and all sorts of techniques—among them techniques of language. . . . Putting this realism into question," he asserts, "is an eminently political act, even if it is not articulated in explicitly political terms, but rather in linguistic and philological ones" (Hamacher, "Journals, Politics," 448, emphasis added).

It is in terms such as these, then, that we can understand Horkheimer's experiment with print journalism as philosophical as well as political in its effects. Hamacher glosses his recollection of the scene further:

> Try to imagine what would happen if daily papers printed news and commentary of three and a half months ago today, if others printed that of fifteen years ago and still others that of 1941, of 1922. The effect would not be to blur past and present, but rather to make them more pronounced. After all, one of the dangerous effects of the chronological order in which newspapers appear is the numbing of the sense of what history, and what the present could be. ("Journals, Politics," 457)

With the stakes thus demonstrably high, there is no time like the present for addressing the dangerous, even deadly, consequences of the failure to reflect on the rhetorical, temporal and ideological conditions of the signals we mistakenly call "live."

§ 4 Missing in action

> It is terrifying to watch Iraq now being readied for mass destruction. First its leader is transformed into the personification of evil, and our new allies the embodiment of virtue. Then Iraq's people and society are reduced to "military assets" in a demonized "Islamic jihad." Finally, after some arbitrary deadline has expired, Iraqi society is declared a virtual nonentity, with cities to be smashed from great distances and heights, agriculture and industry to be torched, roads and bridges to be reduced to rubble. In all this, Western ignorance of Arab and Islamic culture becomes a useful mode of warfare: the enemy is easily dehumanized and readied for the final blow.
>
> —Edward Said, *New York Times*, January 11, 1991

Part of our task of analysis in the aftermath—which might better be termed a wake (Weber, *Mass Mediauras*, 133 ff.)—of the war in the Persian Gulf is to specify the role of the media, and particularly of television,[1] in the double process outlined by Said early in the conflict's first phase, a process that appears contradictory only if we too quickly subsume its rhetoric to an oppositional logic: On the one hand, we have witnessed the *personification* whereby a complex configuration of forces, both discursive and nondiscursive, is given human shape, embodied in an individual, thereby opening the way to the thorough psychologizing and demonizing that in itself constituted a kind of media ground war in 1991 (figured, for example, in the Saddam Hussein masks hurried into production for Carnival in Rio, or again in the ad appearing in the sports pages of the *New York Times* on February 19, 1991, for "Saddam Hussein printed golf-balls," produced by "Specialties Inc.," whose copy exhorted readers to "Enjoy driving that face 300 yards. Excellent gift. Take out your frustration" [B12]).[2] The rhetorical embodiment of evil has had the considerable effect, in *Times* reporter Thomas L. Friedman's symptomatic formulation, of "providing a moral clarity for many Americans unlike anything since the war against Hitler . . . to justify and shape their foreign policy" ("Desert Fog," 4:1).[3] On the other hand,

Said alludes to the *dehumanization* of the Iraqi populace, a process that allows the mass destruction of human life to be translated as a side effect of war. This dehumanization is predicated on Western ignorance of Iraq's culture, an ignorance sanctioned and perpetuated by the media as well as the military, both operating at great distances and heights.[4] We have to reflect, then, on the particular distances of time and space that characterize the structures and effects of the media through which this process is realized.

The precision technology that quickly became a hallmark of the war presents itself as, among other things, an ultimate technology of visibility: the night-vision lenses and infrared radar screens that turn night into day, reducing time differences to a strange sameness, would be cases in point. Another would be the so-called "smart" missile—smart not least because it provides its own footage, the bomb's-eye view, as it does the work of destruction. It provides, that is, what Dan Rather (for one) proudly and repeatedly termed "more remarkable video" (CBS *Evening News*, January 21, 1991) for future release by the Defense Department and for future broadcast by media in the service of power.[5] (Those inclined to dismiss the latter thesis, or to read the service in question as merely a figure, might consult the *New York Times*'s reporting on the entry of coalition forces and the press into Kuwait City: "One man, standing through the sunroof of his car, waved an American flag he had made out of old pajamas and refused to heed a Kuwaiti military man's advice to stop blocking traffic when he stopped to talk to a reporter. 'We give special thanks to Mr. Bush and all the allies: the British, the French, the Egyptians, CNN,' he said" (Lorch, "For a Jubilant Crowd," A6).[6] So much for Canada's vital "sweep and escort" contribution to the allied effort. On the same page ran the report of the surrender of a stranded Iraqi unit to an Italian television crew: "Twenty-five prisoners in one day—talk about the power of the press. In a long and unrewarding campaign, it was one of the few outright victories for television in the Gulf" ["Iraqis surrender to Italian TV," A6].)

In the smart bomb, which Judith Butler, in a lecture at York University on January 24, 1991, termed an "optical phallus,"[7] the technology of destruction and that of reproduction are coimplicated: Saturation bombing meets with saturation coverage, the latter taking us in our living rooms right up to the moment of the target's—and the image's own—dissolution. In fact, of course, this technology participates in rendering that moment—the event in question—*invisible* (and is thus, not incidentally, a near-perfect instrument of censorship). The event is missing in action, and its reporting is complicit with the Defense Department's insistence that minimal collateral damage has taken place—a claim patently false, of the order of disinformation. The technology's effective performance coincides with an effective failure of representation—in George Bush's phrase for the last-ditch Iraqi peace initiative, a cruel hoax indeed. (It may be worth noting parenthetically in this context the irony in CBS's coverage of the early mobilization of protesters across the street from the White House. Dan Rather advised his viewers that the nuts-and-bolts technology of the wide angle was, for reasons he failed to specify, unavailable to the crew covering the first gatherings in Lafayette Park after Bush's January 16 speech and that any estimate of numbers would be unreliable in the absence of "what we in the business call the wide shot" [CBS News, January 16, 1991]. Other relevant figures, however, were soon forthcoming. In terms of absolute numbers, Bush's address was, at the time, the most-watched television broadcast in U.S. history: 65 million of 93 million American TV households tuned in, putting the speech well in front of its runner-up, the concluding episode of *MASH* in 1983. Thus the onset of one war edged out the end of another in the annals of televisual history.[8])

Hoax and disinformation are suggestively linked in an instance provided by the *Oxford English Dictionary* for the sense of the former as "an act . . . of deception, usually taking the form of something fictitious or erroneous, told in such a manner as to impose upon the credulity of the victim." The example is from Trollope's *He Knew He Was Right*: "The people who bring you the news have probably hoaxed you." As a further example of journalistic disinformation, we might consider the report on the destruction of the Al Makat mosque in Basra, Iraq, broadcast February 19, 1991, on

ABC's *World News Tonight.* Peter Jennings's introduction to the story cited 244 bombing raids overnight, 65 of them on civilian targets. In the next breath, he noted that "allied commanders deny any intentional bombing of civilian targets." Correspondent John Martin went on to report that Pentagon officials "actually produced a photograph"—and one wonders what went into the production of this ocular proof—to dispute a claim by the Iraqis that allied bombs damaged the Basra mosque. After an internal debate, the Defense Department determined to broadcast its own claim, backed by sketches of satellite images and by an aerial reconnaissance photograph especially commissioned for the occasion. ABC obliged with file footage, so indicated, of a reconnaissance plane taking off to get the job done—an image produced purely to satisfy the medium's imperative of televisibility.[9] Viewers watched the Defense Intelligence Agency's briefing officer, Rear Admiral Mike McConnell, pointing to these commissioned images, advising where to look, how to read the drawing and photograph as proof positive of the allied counterclaim that Iraqi workers removed the dome of the mosque and then deliberately set demolition charges to simulate the effects of a direct hit, though the bomb had actually landed a hundred yards away.

ABC's reporter dutifully conveyed the response of an Iraqi diplomat who called the Defense Department claim "disinformation" and who posed a question whose rhetorical status is worth pondering: "Why would anyone want to dismantle a mosque?" "The Pentagon stands by its story," concluded correspondent Martin, who clearly stood by his as well. Shortly afterward came reports by delegations visiting Iraq to assess civilian casualties and damage. Ramsay Clark was among those who published their findings: "Basra was the most heavily damaged place we visited. In five residential areas that we examined, hundreds of houses had been destroyed, several hundred people had been killed and many hundreds injured." And he noted that "On the outskirts of Basra the Al Makat mosque lay in rubble; its minaret stood nearby. Ten bodies of the twelve family members believed to have been there when the bomb hit had been found" ("War Crime," 308–9). Belatedly, the dead and injured bodies rendered invisible and practically unthinkable by these precision technologies were accounted for.

Again, it is crucial to reflect on broadcast television as the primary medium in which this information, this disinformation, was relayed. In "Information, Crisis, Catastrophe," Mary Ann Doane writes of the specificity of televisual information, that it

> would seem to be particularly resistant to analysis given its protean nature. . . . television news provide[s] a seemingly endless stream of information, each bit (as it were) self-destructing in order to make room for the next. . . . Information, unlike narrative, is not chained to a particular organization of the signifier or a specific style of address. Antithetical modes reside side by side. Hence, information would seem to have no formal restrictions—indeed, it is characterized by its very ubiquity. If information is everywhere, then the true scandal of *disinformation* in the age of television is its quite precise attempt to *place* or to *channel* information—to direct its effects [I would argue that in the example at hand, this is figured in the insistent *pointing* of the briefing officers, the retired military strategists, and the anchors themselves]. Even if it is activated through television, it uses broadcasting in a narrowly conceived way. Disinformation loses credibility, then, not only through its status as a lie but through its very directedness, its limitation, its lack of universal availability. The scandal is that its effects are targeted. (224)[10]

Disinformation's effects, like the smart missile's, are targeted (if imperfectly destined), only in this case it is we, news junkies and "war potatoes," who are in the crosshairs.[11] Disinformation, Doane argues, "abuses the system of broadcasting by invoking and exploiting the automatic truth value associated with this mode of dissemination—a truth value not unconnected to the sheer difficulty of verification and the very entropy of information" (224).

Once again, the automatic truth value Doane invokes is predicated on our investments in so-called "live" television, investments mobilized to incalculable effect in TV coverage of the Gulf War. In mainstream broadcast journalism (to be distinguished from the work of video activist groups including Deep Dish and Paper Tiger), the televisual imaginary outlined by Stephen Heath and

Gillian Skirrow in "Television: A World in Action" has been exploited in both its aspects: the generalized fantasy that the image is *direct* (functioning as if it were not a technology of representation but somehow an unmediated presentation that would render analysis moot) and *direct for me* (as if it were addressed to me, here and now, by an other *of myself*, in the familiar guise of the evening news anchor). It is crucial to resist the seductions of this generalized fantasy and to recall in particular the temporality of "live" news broadcasting, "the complex interplay of image and sound that makes the news prerecorded even as it goes out live" (Taubin, "No News," 55). What the example of the Basra mosque may help us think is the way in which the missing event takes place in a past—a then and there, however proximate—that will never have existed in the present of the "live" broadcast.

§ 5 Fast-forward

Media reports of the resumption of hostilities between the United States and Iraq in early September 1996 serve to open up what appears as a parenthetical remark in Chapter 4, "Missing in action": The flag-waving witness's inclusion of CNN in his grateful enumeration of the allied forces arrayed against Iraq in 1991 and the journalistic observation that an Iraqi unit's surrender to an Italian television crew constituted "one of the few outright victories for television in the Gulf" ("Iraqis Surrender to Italian TV," A6). For coverage of the American military strikes against Iraq in the wake of Saddam Hussein's reassertion of authority in Kurdish-controlled areas in the north relied heavily on the ideological groundwork carried out more than five years earlier in the broadcast media. This time, viewers encountered "Saddam" (generally referred to in portentous tones by policymakers and commentators only by his sadistic- and satanic-sounding first name) within a frame of reference that was already firmly in place. Press reports commonly cited Jerrold Post of George Washington University, who since 1991

> has painted the dominant perception in Washington of the Iraqi leader. A psychiatrist who spent 21 years with the U.S. Central Intelligence Agency, he became director of the political psychology program at George Washington University in 1986 and, during the gulf

> war, testified before Congress with a psychological profile of Mr. Hussein.
>
> At that time, Dr. Post described Mr. Hussein as suffering from malignant narcissism—a personality disorder consisting of sadism, paranoia, lack of remorse and a grandiose view of self—and being consumed by dreams of glory. (Fraser, "U.S. Launches," A1)

The figure who reappeared in Iraqi state television footage translated and rebroadcast by CNN was thus no stranger to the network's audience, as journalists were quick to observe:

> There was Mr. Hussein again . . . , smiling in grainy Iraqi television footage (was this some bad rerun from the 1991 gulf war days?) as he declared victory against the United States and vowed to retaliate against American interests, even as President Clinton was declaring on American television that Iraq had been punished by American military power. There, too, were the national security aides from the Bush Administration again, defending their unfinished war and selectively reinterpreting history in the process.
>
> Toppling Mr. Hussein was never part of the war plan, and who's to say anyone else would have been better, said Colin Powell, the wartime chairman of the Joint Chiefs of Staff. "I have never quite seen a Saddam Jefferson Hussein standing in the wings, ready to come out and be a democrat," he told CNN. . . .
>
> Fast forward to the Clinton years. The events of last week were an unwelcome reminder that the Clinton team has done no better than the Bush team at reaching (or even defining) its long-term goals in Iraq. (Sciolino, "Staying Power," 4:1)

General Powell, who just weeks before his televisual pronouncement left off "standing in the wings" and was ready to "come out" as a Republican—indeed, as a featured speaker at the party's national convention in San Diego (his role may explain his tacit alignment-by-denegation of Saddam with the capital-D Democrat William Jefferson Clinton, as well as his pointed omission of any mention of Saddam's elite Republican Guard), an event that received "gavel-to-gavel coverage" on CNN—was one of the familiar figures summoned to the screen for the occasion. Subsequent reports identified the party that was in fact "standing in the wings" in northern Iraq:

> Saddam Hussein's attack on the northern Kurdish region of Iraq uncovered a six-year, CIA-funded operation to destabilize the Iraqi government and led to the arrest and apparent execution of more than 100 Iraqis associated with the effort.
>
> It had been the largest covert operation by the CIA since the Afghan War, senior Clinton administration officials said yesterday. And its ending drove the United States back to square one in its effort to remove the Iraqi dictator. . . .
>
> "This is one of the greatest setbacks U.S. intelligence has ever suffered," a senior U.S. official said. ("Saddam Smashes," A12)

Just as familiar to many viewers were the faces of CNN news anchor Bernard Shaw and correspondent Peter Arnett, who, along with their colleague John Holliman, provided the first "live" coverage of the Gulf War in January 1991.[1] Initially over an open audio line, and then via satellite from their Baghdad hotel, CNN's correspondents commenced broadcasting two minutes after the bombing campaign began at 6:33 EST on January 16, and were on the air for an uninterrupted 36 hours (during which viewers heard Shaw, whose photograph was superimposed over a map of Iraq along with the "CNN Live" logo, impart such memorable lines as "Clearly I've never been there, but it feels like we're in the center of hell" and "It has to be pretty unique in journalistic history to have a front row seat"). Their part in vaulting CNN to ascendancy over the established broadcast networks was unabashedly recalled and celebrated in January 1996 during CNN's self-congratulatory programming marking the five-year anniversary of the Gulf War (as Arnett attested, "We made history and became famous").[2] On the morning of September 3, 1996, viewers saw Bernard Shaw at the anchor desk in Washington taking advantage of a telephone interview with Iraqi Deputy Prime Minister Tariq Aziz to negotiate Arnett's re-entry into a city once again under threat of attack with the American expansion of the southern no-fly zone to the suburbs of Baghdad. Shaw interrupted Capitol Hill correspondent Charles Bierbauer's interview with Congressman Lee Hamilton and Senator Richard Lugar to introduce Tariq Aziz "live from Baghdad now." Aziz first provided an update on Iraqi troop movements in the north: "First of all about the existence of the troops in Irbil—our troops have returned to their previous positions fully several hours ago and before the aggression started. Our statements about our intention to withdraw were genuine and correct and all neutral observers in the region have supported that, telling that our troops are still there in the city of Irbil and around the city of Irbil, is unfortunately incorrect and a deliberate disinformation."[3] Strategically, Aziz posed his challenge to alleged American disinformation in terms that affirmed the persuasive power of his medium: "So, there has been an organized campaign of disinformation and misinformation, a deliberate one, to give an excuse to an unjustified military aggression by the United States. We did not violate international law, we did not violate United Nations resolutions and I challenge any representative in the American administration to appear on television and tell the American public and the international public opinion upon what—what basis in international law on what provisions in the Security Council resolution this aggression was based and justified." Shaw, in turn, lost little time in turning the conversation to what he called "a housekeeping question":

> CNN's Correspondent Peter Arnett is standing by in Amman, Jordan. He wants very much and we want very much for him to travel the 15 hours it takes to get from Amman to Baghdad. Will he be given permission to enter your capital and your country?
>
> *Tariq Aziz*: Well . . . I'm—I'm a frank man. I was not very pleased with the CNN coverage of the situation because our statement and our point of view was not—was not very well and even-handedly presented to the American public and to the international public opinion. And so we thought that the presence of Mr. Arnett in Baghdad would not add a lot [unintelligible]. If he is going to help in presenting the real picture to the American public, to the international public opinion, why not? He has been here in very difficult times in the past, you were here, also, Mr. Shaw, and all your colleagues and at CNN were welcome in the past. If you promise that you will give a candid, objective, fair coverage of the situation, then you are welcome.
>
> *Bernard Shaw*: Mr. Minister, as a professional journalist, as an employee of CNN, and as a colleague of Peter Arnett, I don't think that

> CNN's objectivity, our candor or our fairness or our sense of balance can be questioned by any government. We have not only had this live interview with you by telephone, but we have been carrying excerpts from President Saddam Hussein. We have no axes to grind, we don't support any particular government. Our only objective is to report fairly and objectively and we would greatly appreciate it if you would give Mr. Arnett and other CNN personnel permission to enter your country so that we can report both sides of the story. Now, sir, if you would please stand by. . . .

Shaw went on to thank Aziz for his patience "as we continue covering this breaking story"—a narrative interrupted by timely reports by weathercaster Flip Spiceland that "Hurricane Fran is changing her strategy" as the storm threatened to make landfall in the American southeast, by updates on the continuing investigation into the crash of TWA's flight 800, and by fresh graphics that superimposed crosshairs over a map of Iraq while a voice-over asserted: "Once again, it's CNN, the place to turn for complete coverage of the strike in the Gulf." Some time later, Shaw resumed contact with Aziz, "again, live, on the telephone line from Baghdad," and the Deputy Prime Minister had some words for Wolf Blitzer, CNN's senior White House correspondent:

> He say that American officials say that they defend or they justify their action on [U.N.] Resolution 688. I have just faxed the text of this resolution to the CNN headquarters and if you be kind enough, I don't want to take the time of the viewers, if you could put it on screen, ask any legal advice of integrity in international law and look at this resolution and if he find any clue that will justify an American military attack on Iraq five years, more than five years after the adoption of that resolution. That's the verification I wanted to make. . . . So, the text of the resolution is on your desk, you can put it on the screen so that the people of the world would look at this and see if they can derive any conclusion that this military aggression is justified according to the letter of that resolution.
>
> *Bernard Shaw*: And the United Nation's Resolution 688 prohibits the president of your country from oppressing his people, that basically is a thumbnail description of that resolution that you're referring to?

> *Tariq Aziz*: Yeah, but we had not done that. We have helped the people in the north upon their request to go to their support because they were under attack from an adventurous faction allying itself with the Iranians, so the situation is completely different than the situation in 1991. (Cited verbatim from transcript of CNN broadcast)

In an exchange full of references to temporality and allusions to the war's first phase "five years, more than five years" earlier, Shaw, like the media-savvy Aziz, was reluctant to "take the time of the viewers"—but rather than make the letter of the text available on screen, he chose to provide his own thumbnail paraphrase of its spirit. Ignoring the fax on his desk, he returned to what was for him the more pressing matter: the question of his colleague's passage to Baghdad and the possibility of "live" reporting from the scene.

> One final question to you, at this moment, we'll be coming back to the Capitol and talking with you as this story unfolds, of course. One final question, it's a very self-serving question. We're concerned about it here at CNN. Can CNN correspondent Peter Arnett and other CNN people waiting to cross the border in Amman, Jordan, proceed to your border and proceed into Baghdad?
>
> *Tariq Aziz*: That is no problem. CNN reporters have always been welcome in Baghdad. It's just a matter of administrative arrangements I'll have to make this afternoon. The minister of information is not in his [unintelligible] and I promise Mr. Jordan that I will handle this matter this evening.
>
> *Bernard Shaw*: Well, I'm sure [unintelligible] Jordan vice president in charge of international coverage has expressed his appreciation and as Peter's colleague, I express my thank you to you and your government also, because it's important that we be able to report both sides of this story, as you understand. Deputy Prime Minister Tariq Aziz, thank you very much, and we'll come back to you later in this day.

If there is something "unintelligible," or at least not immediately apparent, in these exchanges, it may have to do with what it means for either Aziz or Shaw to "take the time of the viewers." For the temporality in question is not the experiential time of the viewing subject, but more fundamentally still the order of time that events themselves take as they take place on television, in the putative present tense staked out by the "live" logo discreetly superimposed over the image. In this instance, the text we saw on the screen's surface was not that of U.N. Resolution 688, but "the little word 'live' electronically pasted over the image" (Dienst, "Still Life," 164), which has become so predominant, even hegemonic, in broadcast news. And as a text, it remains to be read, which entails interrogating its rhetorical mode and its referential authority:

> The innumerable writings that dominate our lives are made intelligible by a preordained agreement as to their referential authority; this agreement is merely contractual, never constitutive. It can be broken at all times and every piece of writing can be questioned as to its rhetorical mode. Whenever this happens, what originally appeared to be a document or instrument becomes a text and, as a consequence, its readability is put in question. This questioning points back to earlier texts and engenders, in its turn, other texts which claim (and fail) to close off the textual field. (de Man, "Allegory (*Julie*)," 204)

In this light, Paul Virilio's claim that the rhetorical force of the "live" image reduces time to a fait accompli, something to which one simply submits, opts out of the responsibility to read the text at hand (*L'écran du desert*, 77–82). If the automatic truth value readily accorded to the live broadcast has a contractual, not a constitutive, basis, the terms of this pact are arguably those of *The Draughtsman's Contract*, enunciated in a stunning speech that draws upon the "ambiguous evidence of an obscure allegory" cited in Peter Greenaway's film, to situate the artist, who is likewise implicated as spectator, "in the space between knowing and seeing," compelled to act in the face of "a certain blindness. Perhaps you have taken a great deal on trust." The responsibility to mistrust attaches to the act of viewing, every time—not so much because "the people who bring you the news have probably hoaxed you" but because only when the viewer assumes that charge can a reading of television take place. Such a reading, of course, takes time. "We do not confirm or verify, like amateur epistemologists, the actual existence of things by checking in with (their representations on) our televisions—no, we simply take the time to watch them happen. This remains the most difficult thing to think about television: what happens there, and when it comes to pass" (Keenan, "Have you Seen Your World Today?", 102). And this responsibility extends beyond the imperatives, attractions, and threats of the live broadcast, and the hectic presumptions they elicit, to the medium's preprogrammed formats.

§ 6 The test of time

In more senses than one, television is all about survival, and the long-running serial *Knots Landing* is nothing if not a case in point.[1] The history of the popular series begins, inauspiciously but symptomatically, with a postponement, a deferred moment of origin: Though the idea for the show was initially developed in 1977, before the advent of the prime-time melodramatic serial (and its subsequent proliferation in *Dynasty* and *The Colbys*, *L.A. Law* and *NYPD Blue*, *Melrose Place* and *Central Park West*), the explicitly middle-class focus of the proposed series gave the programmers at CBS pause. According to David Jacobs, *Knots Landing*'s creator and co–executive producer, the network was hesitant about undertaking the project and eventually asked for "something on the same order, only glossier, more sensational, easier to promote—more saga than serial" (Introduction, viii). What they got—*Dallas*—fit the bill, and on the strength of its success, the idea for *Knots Landing* was then retrieved "from a bottom drawer" and spun off the hit series that on ideological grounds had displaced it in the conceptual stage. Jacobs recounts further that "if the truth be told, *Knots Landing* was never comfortable as a *Dallas* spin-off. Its aggressive middle-classedness always got in the way." Partly as a result, he suggests, "*Knots Landing* had trouble making ends meet for a while. Though never a failure, it wasn't a success, either; it just hung in, with no identity of its own, either ignored in the press or seen as

Dallas's tagalong little brother who could never live up. [The figuration here alludes to the status of Gary Ewing, the younger brother initially situated on *Dallas* and subsequently transplanted, with his wife Valene, to become one of the four couples on the *Knots Landing* cul-de-sac.] Still, it did what it had to do to get along; it was a survivor" (Jacobs, Introduction, viii). What the series had to do to survive, and specifically to survive its scheduling opposite the formidable *Hill Street Blues*, "the most celebrated television show of its time," is, again according to Jacobs, to "tell some pretty un-middle-class stories"—a story in itself (viii). But *Knots Landing* exemplifies as well another order of survival on and of television, one that is not so much a function of ratings wars but rather of certain of the medium's conditions of possibility and impossibility.

A reference point for this claim would be the series' 200th and 201st episodes ("Noises Everywhere," Parts I and II), which received a good deal of press when they were first aired on December 3 and 10, 1987, because of their experimental character. In what *TV Guide* termed a "risky and unusual proceeding," the actors were called on to improvise over two days, with a sound crew and four cameras recording sixteen hours of videotape, as the basis for the script to follow (Littwin, "Flying," 6). In an exercise coproducer Larry Kasha compared to "going to an analyst," the characters wrote their own story before the fact (Littwin, "Flying," 7).[2] The episodes in question turn around the funeral of Laura Murphy Avery Sumner (whose very name narrates a history of marriage, divorce, and remarriage typical of the melodramatic serial), a long-standing member of this southern California community that her ex-husband Richard Avery (played by sometime writer and director John Pleshette), returning for the occasion after a four-year absence from the show, sardonically calls "a veritable utopia, the solar system's ideal community." That community is metonymically based, comprised as it is of the adjacent lots in a real estate development, and the spatial metonymy has its temporal counterpart in the narrative succession, the "one damn thing after another" of the serial format. According to the account in Laura Van Wormer's *Knots Landing: The Saga of Seaview Circle*, a volume that invents a collective genealogy for the town and its inhabitants, it is also a community whose history is an ongoing struggle for survival: "Like the Native Americans who lived here over two hundred years ago," we read, "the [neighboring families] have placed their faith in communal intimacy as the best defense between them and the dangers of the world at large. For the Native Americans, their way of life could not withstand the pressures from the outside ["along with their culture and technology, the missionaries also brought smallpox and venereal disease with them. The Native Americans had no resistance against these imported diseases and their village was nearly wiped out"]; for the neighbors of Seaview Circle, theirs is undergoing the test of time" (Van Wormer, *Knots Landing*, 3, 6).[3] In the episodes immediately preceding the improvised wake and funeral, Laura (Constance McCashin) fails the test of time imposed on the cul-de-sac: She confronts her own dead end with the discovery that she is fatally ill with brain cancer. (It is worth remarking here that for roughly half of the show's eleven seasons, Laura experienced the living death of the "downtrodden housewife"—her self-description and a memory inscribed in the aftermath of this other death.)[4] In a decision viewed by her family and friends as a violation of the social contract that sustains the close-knit community, Laura determines to leave town to die alone at a clinic in remote Minnesota, even though, as the recriminating Richard angrily points out, "she could have died here."[5] The "here" is of course doubly deictic, indicating at once here *in* Knots Landing and here *on Knots Landing*. For Laura's vexing decision dictates an apparent violation of the diegetic contract as well, in that the viewer is deprived of the pivotal event of her death, which in this episode is registered third-hand in her husband Greg Sumner's report of a phone call from the clinic. To all the mourners' predictable questions about whether she was in much pain at the end, and so on, the taciturn Sumner (played by William Devane) can only reply, "I don't know. I wasn't there." More to the point, because Laura dies in absentia, off camera, they and we miss out on one of the sustaining rituals of soap narrative, whereby a death affords the occasion for the living, the survivors, to address the dead, to say what for one reason or another they couldn't or wouldn't say when it could still be heard and understood, when it could elicit a response. This ritual apostrophe to the dead typically serves a double function: It reaffirms the prevailing values of family and of a certain community, and it provisionally reconciles past differences as an opening onto the projected future of the serial succession. In the radical rewriting of this convention that takes place here, there is, crucially, no body to apostrophize:[6] Laura's remains, we learn, are due to arrive air freight; the wake is prolonged as the flight is delayed, and the body is then delivered to the wrong mortuary. It is rather a spectral, disembodied Laura who returns to address her survivors, and her medium of choice is the videocassette.[7]

The televisual scene of mourning is already haunted by the revenant who takes up residence in the VCR. The ghost in this machine is not only conjured; she herself conjures, exercising her own remote control over her survivors from another time and place. And the figure, the fiction of address, the reverse apostrophe from before and beyond the grave, fatally cuts into the specular system of mimetic representation on which the series, like others of its kind, is predicated. All this warrants analysis, a loosening of the tangled threads of a knot.

Greg Sumner's prefatory announcement to the gathered mourners that "Laura left some farewell messages on a videotape—I'm gonna go in the den and play it" is disconcerting and provokes an unease reflected in the question posed by Richard (who, having in an earlier episode held Laura hostage at gunpoint in their living room and subsequently abandoned her and their two children, may have something to fear): "What *kind* of messages?" Sumner replies with an offhand prediction—"Don't worry, you'll survive"—that is hardly a guarantee and is ironically undercut in the frames that follow, in which he leans against the den wall next to the display case containing his firearms collection with a gun pointed directly at his head. In what sense, then, do they or don't they (and we, who are likewise addressees) survive this scene?

That the rhetoricity of the apostrophe from the dead does not

FIGURE 1. Freeze-frame, Laura's video image, from *Knots Landing* episodes broadcast December 3 and 10, 1987, on CBS.

FIGURE 2. Freeze-frame, Sumner with guns to head, from *Knots Landing* episodes broadcast December 3 and 10, 1987, on CBS.

afford consolation to the living is evident in what happens as Laura's video image addresses, one after another, her survivors. The women—Val (Joan Van Ark), Abby (Donna Mills), and Karen (Michelle Lee)—are apparently spellbound, rendered speechless, capable at most of inarticulate laughter and tears, and one could impute something like a mute recognition on their part that Laura is irrevocably gone, that she can know nothing of what takes place in her memory. In rhetorical terms, what confers the power of speech on the absent, the dead—the figure of prosopopoeia—seems symmetrically to allow for the survivors' being struck dumb, frozen in a freeze-frame that may be understood to prefigure their own deaths.[8] The limit of their subjectivity as spectators is marked out even as that subjectivity is constituted in and by the address, which is at once its condition of possibility and impossibility. It is as if Laura says not "you'll survive" or even "you survive" but "you are dead," "it's *your* funeral, for it is you who have (much to answer for and) nothing to say."

In the speechless figures of Val, Abby, and Karen, the viewer is simultaneously made responsible and unable to respond. That simultaneity is itself an effect of a more differentiated temporal structure, that of the prerecorded, whereby the dead woman dictates, in advance, what her survivors do here and now. In this instance, the then and there of the recorded moment is divided from the viewing present by a death that renders the past absolutely past, its anteriority determinant but irrecoverable. If death is this episode's theme (as is suggested when Sumner asks Jill Bennett, a guest at the post-funeral reception, "Enjoying the party?" and she responds: "You might try a different theme next time"), it has a nonthematic, a syntactic function as well: It marks a rupture, a disjunction in time that is itself unavailable as an event, unthinkable as a present. It is this unavailability, then, that is figured in Laura's decision to go away to die and the perplexity and resistance it prompts. The responses of the female mourners, muted as if by the dead woman's remote control, signal in part that the past of the prerecorded, the already written, cannot be assimilated to the present, cannot be appropriated as cognition (by way of a reinscription of this tropology

FIGURE 3. Freeze-frame, Valene addressed by Laura's image, from *Knots Landing* episodes broadcast December 3 and 10, 1987, on CBS.

FIGURE 4. Freeze-frame, Valene's nonresponse, from *Knots Landing* episodes broadcast December 3 and 10, 1987, on CBS.

of the subject in a specular mode of knowledge) or as memory (on a Hegelian or a Freudian model of recollection as an idealizing, internalizing *Erinnerung*). The viewing subject's predicament, then, is that the other—the other as the other who can die—will always already have spoken, will have had the last word. In effect, the subject has to respond but cannot, is already indebted with no possibility of repayment.[9]

Unlike his fellow survivors, Sumner responds to his wife's farewell message to him (which he withdraws to watch in private) by seeking to engage her video image in a kind of dialogue that would replicate their characteristic Tracy-and-Hepburn repartee (Laura: "You were the only one who made me feel truly loved. Of course you had a weird way of doing it, but it worked." Greg: "I laughed at your dumb jokes"). His mode of response thus figures a resistance to his responsibility, to the debt owed to the other, its priority and unanswerability. Given this departure from the women's mute recognition in the earlier scene (and given Richard's response to Laura's offer of and request for forgiveness, the "I got off easy" with which her first husband seeks to disengage himself from his obligation to her memory), it is perhaps tempting to speak in this connection of a specifically male subjectivity, characterized by the narcissistic effort to domesticate the other's alterity, to appropriate it as meaning, to cast the other as the other *of* a self, of me, myself ("Why'd you leave me all alone? I can't figure why you left me all alone," Greg implores, as Laura's image refuses to take part in the dialogue he attempts to script, and he senses himself losing control; or again, in his words of farewell, "I love you, I hope I don't end up hating you")—even though the death of the other is arguably what constitutes that relation of self to self that we call subjectivity. The asymmetry of an impossible passage (between the dead and the living, between then and now), reflected in the asymmetricalizing of the shot/reverse shot structure in the scene that records this nonexchange, yields noncomprehension (Greg: "You left me in a bad spot, Red. I don't know what you're trying to tell me"), the outcome of the attempt to negotiate the nonnegotiable, to dialogize, dialectize the radical heterogeneity that com-

FIGURE 5. Freeze-frame, Sumner viewing Laura's videotape, from *Knots Landing* episodes broadcast December 3 and 10, 1987, on CBS.

FIGURE 6. Freeze-frame, Sumner's grief, from *Knots Landing* episodes broadcast December 3 and 10, 1987, on CBS.

prises the irreducible predicament of the viewing subject. The inscription of sexual difference here is complicated by the fact that the gender lines in *Knots Landing* (which in the words of Ted Shackelford, the actor who plays Gary Ewing, is "centered on the women" [Littwin, "Flying," 10])[10] are unstable, volatile, more like test patterns, crossing and recrossing, tying themselves in knots.[11] To put it all too quickly and crudely, the mystification is not complete: If the bereaved male subject goes wrong here, in a sense he also gets it right. The movement from his confident "Let's see what you've got to say for yourself" as he activates the VCR to the surrender of "Whatever you say" as he begins to break down, reduced to mute, tearful nodding at the image, traces the impossibility of making the other speak without the other's having already spoken and having said something other than what is given to be seen and understood. The other speaks otherwise, in a mode that may be generalizable as an allegory of television.

Once again, Stephen Heath and Gillian Skirrow's formulation is instructive: "What is specific to television—the possibility of 'live broadcasting,' the present electronic production of the image—becomes the term of its exploited imaginary, the generalized fantasy . . . that is, that the image is direct, and direct for me . . . which fantasy . . . is then taken for the ground reality of television and its programs" ("Television").[12] What is perhaps ironic in the instance of *Knots Landing* is that a certain resistance to this generalized fantasy turns up in the fantasy factory of melodramatic serial television, which demystifies even as it exploits that imaginary in both its aspects: "that the image is direct" (functioning as if it were not a technique of representation, but somehow an unmediated presentation that would render analysis moot) "and direct for me" (as if it were addressed to me by an other of myself). As well, the series relies on a mimetic mode of representation, yet, in scenes such as those in which Laura's image addresses and implicates her mourners, affords a locus of resistance to its easy seductions. To this extent, Jacobs (together with die-hard fans) may be justified in the claim for *Knots Landing*'s "difference" from other serials developed after 1979, though that difference would not reside in its putatively middle-class content, which in any case lapsed over the course of the program's history. Its difference would instead be a function of the relative adequacy of its response to "the question everybody raise[s] . . . of knowing how to introduce resistance into this cultural industry. I believe," pursues Jean-François Lyotard, "that the only line to follow is to produce programmes for TV, or whatever, which produce in the viewer or the client in general an effect of uncertainty and trouble. . . . You can't introduce concepts, you can't produce argumentation. This type of media isn't the place for that, but you can produce a feeling of disturbance, in the hope that this disturbance will be *followed* by reflection" ("Brief Reflections," 58; emphasis added).

The possibility that the telepitaphic allegory relayed in Laura's disturbing video apostrophe haunts all TV, even and especially so-called "live broadcasting," is figured in advance early in Part I of the same episode, in a scene in which Mack Mackenzie searches for words to console his old friend Sumner on the loss of his wife. The expression of sympathy finds its form in a question: "What's the point in being Irish, right?" Sumner's noncomprehending "What?"—an interrogative that punctuates the *Knots* syntax at frequent intervals—elicits an elaboration on Mack's part: "I don't think there's any point in being Irish if you don't know that the world is going to break your heart some day." Greg's reply, "If you say so," anticipates the "Whatever you say" he later directs to Laura's video image and prompts Mack to mark his unmarked quotation: "Daniel Patrick Moynihan said so, after JFK was shot." Sumner: "Sounds like he was sitting around waiting for it to happen." Mack: "What?" Sumner: "Waiting for his heart to get broken."[13]

As a slew of twenty-fifth-anniversary broadcasts and rebroadcasts served to remind, the assassination and funeral of "the first television President" are for several generations of viewers (American, but not only American) paradigmatic of the televisual event brought "live" to us in our living rooms. The notion that Moynihan and we with him were somehow "sitting around waiting for it to happen" confirms that the death of the other takes place, so to speak, before the event, in a past that will never have existed in the present of the "live" broadcast and in a way that marks us out, in advance, as subjects. The funeral—Laura's, JFK's—stages the scene of mourning from which televisual discourse and spectator subjectivity cannot escape but which they nevertheless, more or less, survive.[14]

PART THREE

Journals of survival

§ 7 "Only a question of time, etc."

(The diary of Alice James)

We begin with a modest claim—or rather with the citation of one: "The diary of Alice James, invalid sister of the psychologist William and of the novelist Henry, represents her modest claim on posterity beside the works of her famous brothers" (Edel, Preface, vii). This claim for Alice James, made in her name, opens Leon Edel's preface to his edition of the journal. The attribution of modesty comes as no surprise and is entirely in keeping with the standard critical apologies for the diary and the surviving letters that, together with her commonplace book, complete this circumscribed body of work, these "thoughtful notes of a daughter and a sister," as Edel calls them in his introduction (22)—in keeping with their devaluation and practically their invalidation on the grounds of their authorship by the invalid younger sister whose "claim to attention" at the time of the journal's first publication in 1934 "was still as an appendage to brothers" (Edel, Preface, viii). The modesty assigned reflects the relegation to marginal status of a corpus that, so the argument goes, pales beside the monumental achievements, scientific and aesthetic, of William and Henry. In generic terms as well, this slight autobiographical oeuvre is taken to mark a decidedly minor event in American letters: Indeed, Alice James's sole publication prior to her death was a letter, an anecdotal note to the editor of *The Nation*, signed "Invalid."

The predictable premises of this relegation to modest, marginal, and minor status have been challenged in more recent interpretations of the journal and letters on the part of Ruth Bernard Yeazell and Raymond Bellour as well as in briefer critical interventions by Mary Jacobus and Jacqueline Rose. Yeazell's introduction to her edition of the letters, for example, tacitly amends Edel's assessment of the diary's modest claim to read: "Alice claims our attention less in spite of her invalidism than because of it, and she claims it with a distinctive Jamesian energy" (5). Critics spanning several generations and theoretical positions thus acknowledge that some claim is being made on posterity, which is to say on our attention as readers, as the diary's posthumous addressees. One of the journal's first readers, Henry James, noted in a letter to William following their sister's death that "her style, her power to write," "constitute (I wholly agree with you) a new claim for the family renown" (Edel, Introduction, 19).[1] But what happens when we interrogate further this rhetoric of claiming, in an attempt to specify the nature, the object and the validity of a demand that is in fact asserted immodestly, with force (Alice James's word is "potency"), and even with a certain "violence" (again, her term), in the pages of the journal? Although Edel (to cite him once more as an instance of a critical commonplace in the accounts of the corpus) notes summarily that "The claim of life against the claim of death—this is the assertion of every page of Alice's diary" (Introduction, 16), a reconsideration of those pages suggests rather that Alice James's diary breaks with the oppositional logic of life against death, and deliberately reinscribes its terms—as it does the same logic brought to bear on the categories of gender and health. The journal disrupts, that is, the very system that would guarantee its relegation (as the private record of a woman's—a daughter's, a sister's—illness) to modest, marginal, minor status in the first place.

Among the crucial junctures in this text that consistently works to preempt its own invalidation is the moment when Alice James's long-awaited death sentence is finally pronounced in no uncertain terms. As Yeazell observes, over the course of more than twenty years of attempted treatments, tentative recoveries and inevitable relapses, the career invalid had weathered a succession of indeterminate diagnoses and impalpable prognoses (*Death and Letters*, 10). The diagnoses ranged from "nervous hyperaesthesia" to "spinal neurosis" (*Diary*, 207) to "an abnormally sensitive nervous organization" (*Death and Letters*, 117) to her mother's judgment around the time of James's first breakdown: "It is a case of genuine hysteria for which no cause as yet can be discovered. It is a most distressing form of illness, and the most difficult to reach, because little is known about it" (*Death and Letters*, 11).[2] The latter diagnosis is problematic in a way that Jacqueline Rose elucidates: "To describe Alice as a[n] hysteric is of course a problem. We can list her constantly redefined and reexperienced ills—paralysis, suppressed gout, cramps of the stomach and what she called cramps of the mind, sick headaches, toppling over and fainting out. But we are forced to acknowledge that, in William James's words, this disease '*with no definite symptoms*' . . . resides, above all, in its designation as hysteria" ("Jeffrey Masson and Alice James," 187).[3] And a long history of prognoses could be summarized by the patient herself: "And then these doctors tell you that you will die, or *recover!* But you *don't* recover. I have been at these alternations since I was nineteen and am neither dead nor recovered—as I am now forty-two there has surely been time for either process" (*Diary*, 142). But between the either/or of the doctors' logical code, an unequivocal diagnosis and prognosis are, in time, delivered:

> To him who waits, all things come! My aspirations may have been eccentric, but I cannot complain now, that they have not been brilliantly fulfilled. Ever since I have been ill, I have longed and longed for some palpable disease, no matter how conventionally dreadful a label it might have. . . . I have been going downhill at a steady trot; so they sent for Sir Andrew Clark four days ago, and the blessed being has endowed me not only with cardiac complications, but says that a lump that I have had in one of my breasts for three months, which has given me a great deal of pain, is a tumour, that nothing can be done for me but to alleviate pain, that it is only a question of time, etc. (*Diary*, 206–7)

Far from occasioning dread or terror, Sir Andrew's "uncompromising verdict," as James terms it, has the salutary effect of "lifting us out of the formless vague and setting us within the very heart of the sustaining concrete" (*Diary*, 207)—the very heart of the concrete cast as "this unholy granite substance in my breast" (*Diary*, 225).[4]

Yet to Alice James, avid reader of George Sand and her "beloved" Jules Lemaître and whose journal is a tissue of citations from the French, "tumour" may well have sounded as a brutal, even if welcome, judgment.[5] For the physician's verdict, addressed to her with a certain familiarity, has a complex rhetorical and temporal status: it tells the truth, *dit la vérité*, accurately *describes* a state of affairs in the present (*tu meurs*, you are dying) while it also *prescribes*, in the tension of this present tense, a future (*tu meurs*, you must die, you shall die). The verdict, then, is also a sentence, a sentencing. And however idiomatic and untranslatable, Alice James hears and understands it as such: In particularizing her ailment, the terrible apostrophe posits the law of her life, a law that, over time, will enforce itself as reference.[6]

This parsing of the cruel diagnosis may help us to bring into focus the outlook afforded in the physician's superfluous gloss, whose very generality of formulation makes it paradigmatic as prognosis.[7] If it is "only a question of time, etc." for Alice James—who lives on, and so on, a long nine months after the verdict is delivered, and before she is delivered to her death—the temporality of the journal (a genre or mode conventionally associated with the present tense, with writing to the moment) consistently surpasses the present, staking in effect a counterclaim against her father's assessment, in his 1853 essay "Woman and the 'Woman's Movement,'" of the "question of time" as it properly pertains to woman: "The very virtue of woman [is] her practical sense, which leaves her indifferent to past and future alike, and keeps her the busy blessing of the present hour."[8] Far from being unmindful of the past and future, Alice James is if anything practically oblivious to the present hour, as she confesses in a letter to William: "It seems sad to think of you with yr. love of kin left alone in Cambridge with the family melted like snow from about you, but our dead are among *les morts qui sont toujours vivants*. Your wife allies you to the present [an allusion, here, to the other Alice, and an echo of the father's thesis] &

your children to the future, but I live altogether in the past, I have a momentary & spasmodic consciousness of the present" (*Death and Letters*, 139).

What, then, are the terms of this preoccupation with the past on James's part? The journal as well as the letters are, first of all, the site of a memory work and its peculiar tropology, in which death figures time and again: the locus of an effort to come to grips with her history in what amounts to a struggle for survival ("What *is* living in this deadness called life," she writes, "is the struggle of the creature in the grip of its inheritance and against the consequences of its acts" [*Diary*, 38]). From the vantage point of a "moment of middle life" that, ironically, will prove much nearer the end, the journal ostensibly seeks to reclaim a sense of the past as a basis for self-understanding: "And what joys of youth equal this blessed moment of middle life, when serene and sure of our direction all the simple incidents of daily life and human complication explain and enrich themselves as they are linked and fitted to the wealth of past experience. Whilst the blank youthful mind, ignorant of catastrophe, stands crushed and bewildered before the perpetual postponement of its hopes, things promised in the dawn that the sunset ne'er fulfils." More specifically, as she goes on to note,

> Owing to muscular circumstances my youth was not of the most ardent, but I had to peg away pretty hard between 12 and 24, 'killing myself,' as some one calls it—absorbing into the bone that the better part is to clothe oneself in neutral tints, walk by still waters, and possess one's soul in silence. How I recall the low grey Newport sky in that winter of 62–3 as I used to wander about over the cliffs, my young soul struggling out of its swaddling-clothes as the knowledge crystallized within me of what Life meant for me, one simple, single and before which all mystery vanished. A spark then kindled which every experience great and small has fed into a steady flame which has illuminated my little journey and which, altho' it may have burned low as the waters rose, has never flickered out—'une pensée, unique éternelle, toujours mêlée a l'heure présente.' How profoundly grateful I am for the temperament which saves from the wretched fate of those poor creatures who never find their bearings, but are tossed like dryed leaves hither, thither and yon at the mercy of every event which o'ertakes

> them. Who feel no shame at being vanquished, or at crying out at the common lot of pain and sorrow, who never dimly suspect that the only thing which survives is the resistance we bring to life and not the strain life brings to us. (*Diary*, 95–96)

The considerable stakes of such a passage are to establish and affirm the continuity of past experience with a present that, while it is not the future projected by the struggling young soul—while it was not to have been predicted—is yet part of a coherent history, and, as such, meaningful. The life lesson recounted here ("one simple, single") seems amenable to a straightforward narrative rendering, to crystallization as knowledge and as memory, on the model of an interiorizing ("within me") and idealizing recollection, or *Erinnerung*. But the meaning ostensibly made available here is not independent of the journal's characteristic figuration, in which, again, death is the presiding trope. Here as elsewhere, the relationship between the text's apparent thematic statement and its rhetorical operation is not simple, single, or straightforward. In this "memory of her youth as an exercise in self-destruction" (Yeazell, *Death and Letters*, 13), Alice James recalls the past in terms of "'killing [her]self,' as some one calls it." Given the elaboration, over the course of what she calls her "mortal career," of her project of "getting myself dead—the hardest job of all," the metaphorical suicide alluded to here is not one figure among others—nor is it simply a figure, given its eventual performativity.[9] If the passage lays claim to continuity, to the possibility of "link[ing] and fit[ting]" past experience to "daily life and human complication" in the present, that continuity rests uneasily upon a tropology of memory that, once again, confuses what we take to be the conditions of life and death. As Alice James goes on to assert, what "survives" the passage from then to now—"the only thing" to do so—is "the resistance we bring to life": a formulation that is itself a locus of resistance in more senses than one.[10]

In his preface to *What Maisie Knew*, Henry James raises "the question of the particular kind of truth of resistance I might be able to impute to my central figure—some intensity, some continuity of resistance being naturally of the essence of the subject"

(10). If a certain "truth of resistance" might be imputed to the figure of the invalid sister, read in the text of her journal, what particular kind would it be? What is being resisted in such a passage, and in the name of what? The syntactical symmetry of the chiasmus—"the only thing which survives is the resistance we bring to life and not the strain life brings to us"—initially suggests that we understand this resistance as a resource, as the force we marshall *in* life, in what Alice James takes to be our "struggle . . . in the grip of [our] inheritance and against the consequences of [our] acts": resistance, then, on the analogy of an attribute of matter, as what keeps it (and us) from being "tossed like dryed leaves . . . at the mercy of every event which o'ertakes" us.[11] The epistemological stakes of such a reading are apparent if we recall the fundamental Aristotelian formulation in which matter becomes cognizable precisely through the resistance it affords; it is through their resistance that we come to know physical objects.[12] Such an understanding is apparently borne out in another symmetrical formulation in the letters: "Surely there is nothing so true as that we are simply at the mercy of what we bring to life and not what life brings to us" (*Death and Letters*, 135).[13] But while Alice James's career is arguably a life of resistance in this sense, the passage in question allows for other readings as well, readings that complicate a response to the question posed in the preface to *Maisie*: "successfully to resist . . . what would that be?" The apparent symmetry afforded by the grammatical figure and the totalizing understanding that chiasmus seems to warrant are upset by the rhetorical opening onto other possible senses, likewise justified by the text. In other words, the grammatical determination of the meaning of the figure leaves something unaccounted for in a version of what William James, in an essay that Alice glosses in the diary, calls an "Unclassified *Residuum*" ("Hidden Self," 90).[14]

For "the resistance we bring to life" might also be read as resistance *to* life, *opposed to* life, in the name of death. Alice James writes that she "aspires" to die (her word), that she lives (and writes) *for* the eventuality of her death, which finally materializes in the anticipated "mortuary moment." Such resistance finds expression in the epitaphic tonality that prevails from early on in the journal (Jacobus, *Reading Woman*, 249). Or again, "the resistance we bring to life" might be thought as the resistance we animate or reanimate, as we might the dead. In this instance, the crucial figure in the rhetoric of memory would be not the grammatical chiasmus but personification or prosopopoeia, which gives "life" to the dead, and hence functions crucially in both autobiographical and epitaphic discourse.[15] In question, then, would be a resistance that language, in its rhetorical function as prosopopoeia, brings, figuratively speaking, to life.[16] Rhetoric thus resists the grammatical decoding of meaning in the language of this formulation, to open up multiple possibilities that call for a reading of this resistance, for reading as the resistance to a determination of sense that would ignore the divergence between the text's grammatical and rhetorical operations.

The scheme just outlined must accommodate a further characteristic complication in the diary passage, for it is not only her own past that is figured in terms of "killing herself" (later she will confess that "The fact is, I have been dead so long and it has been simply such a grim shoving of the hours behind me as I faced a ceaseless possible horror" [*Diary*, 230]). Indeed, the very pastness of the past is figured by death, and more specifically, figured in the person of the dead friend, the dead parent, conjured like a ghost to haunt the text: for example, in a recollected scene of reading that opens onto another encounter with the past. The journal entry for January 29, 1890, begins with James's ironic venting of her irritation at being overlooked by a flu epidemic; since "there is no hope of my sowing a microbe," she writes, it seems death is to be postponed yet again. "My being, however," she goes on to recount,

> has been stirred to its depths by what I might call ghost microbes imported in my Davenport which came from home ten days ago. In it were my old letters. I fell upon Father and Mother's and could not tear myself away from them for two days. One of the most intense, exquisite and profoundly interesting experiences I ever had. I think if I try a little and give it form its vague intensity will take limits to itself, and the 'divine anguish' of the myriad memories stirred grow less.

> Altho' they were as the breath of life to me as the years have passed they have always been as present as they were at first and [will be for] the rest of my numbered days, with their little definite portion of friction and serenity, so short a span, until we three were blended together again, if such should be our spiritual necessity. But as I read it seemed as if I had opened up a post-script of the past and that I had had, in order to find them *truly*, really to lose them. . . . Mother died Sunday evening, January 29th, 1882, Father on Monday midday, December 19th, 1882, and now I am shedding the tears I didn't shed then! (*Diary*, 78–79)[17]

The formalizing gesture in this passage ("I think if I try a little and give it form") corresponds to the stated function of the journal more generally as one of imposing limits on the flux, the "vague intensity" of recollected experience (formalization is also, as we have seen, the effect of the doctor's diagnosis, the verdict—"tumour"—that releases Alice from the "formless vague"). The scene of reading intervenes to transform a more complacent sense of the past expressed earlier in the diary: "Mr Howells letter made me so happy by saying that mine had made mother and father seem living to him. No greater happiness can come than finding that they survive, or can be *re*-vived, in a few memories" (*Diary*, 32–33). But what survive, what are revived with the opening of the Davenport, are mere "ghost microbes," so many phantom proxies whose resistance to appropriation by bereaved memory (and even by Alice's "floating-particle sense" [*Diary*, 51]) is a function of their virtual immateriality as well as their ephemerality. Once again, the journal's turn of phrase breaks with the oppositional logic of life versus death: The microbes are indeed death-bearing, but the death in question is one that animates, enlivens the invalid reader.

If reading these phantomized missives, addressed to her from before and beyond the grave, seems to open up a postscript of the past, it may be that reading (and writing) the past can only take place as such an afterthought, whose relation to that past is allegorical, alluding to an anteriority that, although determinant for our "momentary and spasmodic consciousness of the present," cannot be recovered as presence, recuperated as knowledge (on the model of the self-knowledge of a self-present, self-identical subject), nor as memory conceived, after Hegel and after Freud, as the internalization of *Erinnerung*. In the belated, postscriptive mourning that takes place here—"now I am shedding the tears I didn't shed then!"—memory comes to terms with a certain otherness, with the radical alterity of the past *as past*, as figured in the dead (in something like the way that, in *The Portrait of a Lady*, it is figured in the absent eyes and alien lips of the Greek statues that Isabel Archer contemplates in Rome[18]). Death divides the living from this past, rendering it absolute, irreducible to any form of presence: a past from which the dead will never return except as revenant, as insubstantial and fleeting phantom proxy; a past to which they are irretrievably lost. The imperative "really to lose" her mother and father is the imperative to leave them (to) their otherness, to abandon the project of mourning as assimilation and prescriptive closure.

All this may help us to read the ways in which the journal inscribes this right of the other to death—its engagement, from early on, in a mourning that would respect the other's infinite remove. Such a respect underlies the passages in which Alice James mocks the mystified memorializing practices of her acquaintances: "Some friend was gushing to K[atharine] over Mrs Charles Kingsley's devotion to the memory of her husband, and gave in proof of it, that she always sat beside his bust and had his photo pinned to the adjoining pillow; as the last expression of refined spiritual sentiment, could anything be more grotesquely loathesome" (*Diary*, 228). Alice James's respect for the memory of her dead—to the extent they can still be termed "hers"—resists the seductions of proximity ("sat beside," "adjoining pillow") and mimetic fidelity ("his bust," "his photo"), taking a different turn:

> Constance Maud told me of her sorrow at some moment when it was thought that her Mother was dying and how she prayed to God to spare her life—the sincerity and strength of the feeling which she showed increased the shocked sense which filled me as I listened. One cries out, bowed down in supplication, for strength, but how can any creature . . . propose to make her paltry necessities an element for the modification of another's destiny. . . . I remember how horrified I was

> to the core of my being when some said to me that in the month when Father lay dying, refusing to eat, that I must urge him and tell him that he must eat for *my sake*!! (*Diary*, 124–25)

The same line of argument appears in the letters as well: "We were so glad," she recalls, "to have him go & that he was not kept in weariness & desolation any longer after Mother's death that we could give no thought to our own loss" (*Death and Letters*, 91).

What amounts to the assertion of a claim to the other's right to a death that no longer, strictly speaking, concerns the living is even more emphatic with respect to Alice's memory of her mother's death, an increasing preoccupation as her own end draws near. In a passage written after the diagnosis of her cancer, Alice reflects that an old friend's consoling words are, at this late stage, beside the point:

> how little all assurances of one's own immortality seem to concern one, now. . . . References to those whom we shall meet again make me shiver, as such an invasion of their sanctity, gone so far beyond, for ever since the night that Mother died, and the depth of filial tenderness was revealed to me, all personal claim upon her vanished, and she has dwelt in my mind a beautiful illumined memory, the essence of divine maternity from which I was to learn great things, give all, but ask nothing. (*Diary*, 220–21)

When all personal claim, on the part of the living, vanishes in the void, no possibility remains of transaction, of reciprocity between the dead and those left to mourn them. Thus Alice reserves special scorn for the figure of the "medium," whose claim to communicate with the dead and gone promises what proves an impossible passage. As she notes in the journal a week before her death,

> It is taken for granted apparently that I shall be spiritualized into a 'district messenger,' for here comes another message for Father and Mother; imagine my dragging them, of whom I can only think as a sublimation of their qualities, into gossip about the little more or the little less faith of Tom, Dick or Harry. I do pray to heaven that the dreadful Mrs. Piper [a famous Boston medium whose career William James researched over a period of twenty years] won't be let loose upon

> my defenceless soul. I suppose the thing 'medium' has done more to degrade spiritual conception than the grossest forms of materialism or idolatry. (*Diary*, 231)

And when William goes so far as to request a lock of Alice's hair to transmit to Mrs. Piper, she is not entirely defenseless, as she subsequently advises him by letter: "I hope you wont be 'offended' . . . when I tell you that I played you a base trick about the hair. It was a lock, not of my hair, but that of a friend of Miss Ward's who died four years ago. I thought it a much better test of whether the medium were simply a mind-reader or not, if she is something more I should greatly dislike to have the secrets of my organisation laid bare to a wondering public" (*Death and Letters*, 106–7). The trick of substituting a lock of another's hair—the friend of a friend, already dead—throws a wrench in the works of a mediation in which she can have no faith.

As this latter passage begins to suggest, Alice James's fierce respect for the right of the other to its difference and its history is bound up with her own sense of self-respect, firmly grounded in a resistance to "invasion" and appropriation. From early on in the journal, she registers shock at such attempts on the part of others unknown to her (to include her prospective reader, whom she addresses as "dear Inconnu" [*Diary*, 129, 166]): "Imagine hearing that someone here in Leamington whom I had never seen had said that I was 'very charitable.' I felt as if all my clothes had been suddenly torn off and that I was standing on the steps of the Town Hall, in the nude, for the delectation of the *British Matron*" (*Diary*, 32). Although this passage registers the modesty, the repressed sexuality of the aging virgin, the threat of violation recounted here may also be understood to call up the corresponding energy of a certain resistance to determining the relation to the other as one of ready reciprocity.

The resistance that Alice James brings to life—the only thing that survives—finds expression in the claim to her right to death as it comes to the other and as it comes to her through the other on whom she renounces all personal claim. If the right to death—the other's and her "own"—is the object of the claim staked by the journal, the rhetoric of claiming must itself respect a temporal imperative whose terms are nonnegotiable. Those terms, which affirm the allegorical structure of memory and mourning, dictate that death cannot take place *now*, but only *then*, in the (recollected) past of the other's death, in the (anticipated) future of one's own. This impossibility imposes itself most forcefully on the text of the journal in its account of the question of suicide, an act that represents the promise of death now, on one's own terms, in one's own time. "I shall proclaim," the invalid writes, "that any one who spends her life as an appendage to five cushions and three shawls is justified in committing the sloppiest kind of suicide at a moment's notice" (*Diary*, 81). This claim to the right to "kill herself" at a moment's notice (and even the time of this notice postpones the fatal moment) asks to be read in relation to another moment, from a time before the journal was undertaken. As her father recollects in a letter to his son Robertson written in 1878, during the period of one of Alice's most severe breakdowns, when she was "half the time, indeed much more than half, on the verge of insanity and suicide,"

> One day a long time ago . . . [she] asked me whether I thought that suicide, to which at times she felt very strongly tempted, was a sin. I told her that I thought it was not a sin except where it was wanton, as when a person from a mere love of pleasurable excitement indulged in drink or opium to the utter degradation of his faculties and often to the ruin of the human form in him; but that it was absurd to think it sinful when one was driven to it in order to escape bitter suffering, from spiritual influx, as in her case, or from some loathsome form of disease, as in others. I told her that so far as I was concerned she had my full permission to end her life whenever she pleased; only I hoped that if she ever felt like doing that sort of justice to her circumstances, she would do it in a perfectly gentle way in order not to distress her friends. She then remarked that she was very thankful to me, but she felt that now she could perceive it to be her right to dispose of her own body when life had become intolerable, she could never do it: that when she had felt tempted to do it, it was with a view to break bonds, or assert her freedom, but that now I had given her freedom to do in the premises what she pleased, she was more than content to stay by my side, and battle in concert with me against the evil that is in the

> world. I dont fear suicide much since this conversation, though she often tells me that she is strongly tempted still. (Yeazell, *Death and Letters*, 15–16)

The temptation "violently [to] discontinue herself," as she elsewhere terms it, meets with an abstract reflection on suicide that culminates in the granting of paternal "permission to end her life whenever she pleased," of "her right to dispose of her own body when life had become intolerable." What is remarkable about the exchange recollected by Henry Sr. is the asymmetry between the question and the answer it prompts: Alice doesn't ask his permission—she rather inquires, with some measure of disinterest, whether suicide is a sin—but she gets it nonetheless. If afterwards, in the father's phrase, "she could never do it," this permanent impossibility may not be simply the effect of a disarming "lack of paternal resistance" that incapacitates the daughter, emptying the tacit threat of its force (Yeazell, *Death and Letters*, 16)—the strong temptation, after all, remains. Once more, a temporal imperative intervenes to postpone the possibility of death. Time and again, Alice James observes the terms of this imperative as she translates them in the journal: "the law that you cannot either escape or hasten the moment" (*Diary*, 161). And in the letters: "the law that you cant hasten the moment, in any development" (*Death and Letters*, 184). The consequences of the doctor's prognosis—"it is only a question of time, etc."—thus unfold in reverse, shedding retrospective light on the text. Those consequences are brought home in another recollection, this time the daughter's of the father (the father who eventually committed the kind of "perfectly gentle" suicide he recommended to Alice, by declining to take nourishment over a period of months after the death of his wife). In another haunting passage from the diary, Alice James confesses, "I can hear, as of yesterday, the ring of Father's voice, as he anathematized some shortcomings of mine in Newport one day: 'Oh, Alice, how hard you are!' and I can remember how penetrated I was, not for the first time,[19] with the truth of it, and saw the repulsion his nature with its ripe kernal of human benignancy felt—alas! through all these years, that hard core confronts me still" (*Diary*, 191).

The recollected ring of the father's apostrophe—"Oh, Alice, how hard you are!"—affords another instance of the complex temporality and rhetoricity we noted in the "uncompromising verdict" pronounced by Sir Andrew Clark. For it is at once descriptive of past and present inadequacies, in an assessment whose truth Alice acknowledges, and uncannily prescriptive, in the grammar of the present, of the future, precisely in the way that it anticipates the verdict, the other terrible apostrophe: "*tu meurs.*" All unknowingly, the father diagnoses in advance the tumour, the "loathsome form of disease" that will catch up with Alice, "that hard core" that eventually materializes in the "unholy granite substance in [her] breast."

A correlate of "the law that you cant hasten the moment, in any development"—the law according to which Alice James's history unfolds—is another imperative, one that demands the renunciation of all personal claim on the other, on the past as figured in the other, that she traces to the death of her mother. In the penultimate entry in the journal, dated six days before her own death, she writes: "How wearing to the substance and exasperating to the nerves is the perpetual bewailing, wondering at and wishing to alter things happened, as if all personal concern didn't vanish as the 'happened' crystallizes into history. Of what matter can it be whether pain or pleasure has shaped and stamped the pulp within, as one is absorbed in the supreme interest of watching the outline and the tracery as the lines broaden for eternity" (*Diary*, 231–32). Calmly confronting her impending death, Alice James renounces all remaining traces of personal concern with the past, and all desire to "alter things happened."[20] And she voids in advance any such concern on the part of her survivors, any claim, however well-meaning, they may seek to make on her history. As she writes to William, "So when I am gone, pray don't think of me simply as a creature who might have been something else had neurotic science been born" (*Death and Letters*, 187). In the ironic mode characteristic of the letters and the journal, sustained unto death, Alice James rejects the modal perfect of the might have been—what her other brother, under the rubric "operative irony," understood as "the possible other case, the case rich and edifying where the actuality is pretentious and vain" (Henry James, *Art of the Novel*, 222).[21] Hers are rather the terms of the verses of Christina Rossetti, cited in a diary entry that goes on to incorporate a newspaper report of the death—by suicide—of a young woman jilted by her lover:

> When I am dead, my dearest,
> Sing no sad songs for me.
> Plant thou no roses at my head
> Nor shady cypress tree.
> Be the green grass above me
> With showers and dewdrops wet;
> And if thou wilt, remember,
> And if thou wilt, forget.
> (*Diary*, 140)

Alice James's rigorous renunciation of the personal as well as the hypothetical, then, extends well beyond the limits of her own case, or any other case in particular. If she begins the diary with the idea of "writing a bit about what happens, or rather doesn't happen" (*Diary*, 25), as the first entry attests, what survives to the last is her absorbing interest in "the 'happened'" as it "crystallizes into history." We might recall here that the career invalid had another profession as well, though it was short-lived: She conducted a correspondence course for the Society to Encourage Studies at Home on the subject of history ("In attempting to teach history," she informs a friend by letter, "I am not half the fool that I look" [*Death and Letters*, 76]). In the history lesson afforded by the journal, the "literary remains" addressed to her survivors ("I feel sorry for you all, for I feel as if I hadn't yet given my message" [*Diary*, 218]), the "outline and the tracery" of the past—of the "happened"—do not assume the shape of a self's history. Situated at the vanishing point of all personal concern, all personal claim, at the limit of appropriation as knowledge or memory, history as "the 'happened'"—as what has occurred, what has taken place—does not appear in any recognizably organic, teleological or dialectical form or as an empty abstraction or generality.[22] It does, however, bear a certain resemblance to allegory, understood as the possibility that permits language, however provisionally, to say the other, to say the past as other, as determinant but irrecoverable for any here and now. And the marginal, minor, invalid historian begins oddly to resemble a figure from the third of Walter Benjamin's "Theses on the Concept of History": "A chronicler who recites events without distinguishing between major and minor ones, acts in accordance with the following truth: nothing that has ever happened should be regarded as lost for history" (254). But the diarist—whose every word could be her last—resists this final attempt at appropriation by resemblance as well, for Alice James writes strictly in accordance with the terms of her own "post-script of the past," terms that respect the other's right to an other history and dictate that the happened—the past as past—should be regarded as lost, "*really*" lost, *to* history.

§ 8 "The only news was when"

(The journals of Derek Jarman)

> The contrast between the continuation not only of [the Verdurins'] existence, but of the fullness of their powers, and the obliteration of so many friends whom I had already seen vanish here or there, gave me the same feeling that we experience when in the stop-press column of the newspapers we read the very announcement that we least expected, for instance that of an untimely death, which seems to us fortuitous because the causes that have led up to it have remained outside our knowledge. This is the feeling that death does not descend uniformly upon all men, but that a more advanced wave of its tragic tide carries off a life situated at the same level as others which the waves that follow will long continue to spare. We shall see later on that the diversity of the forms of death that circulate invisibly is the cause of the peculiar unexpectedness of obituary notices in the newspapers.
>
> —Marcel Proust, *Remembrance of Things Past*

If in Proust's account the obituary announcement of an untimely death exemplifies the unexpected, a remarkable editorial in one newspaper in particular may afford, well after the fact, a gloss on Marcel's experience in *Remembrance of Things Past.* Under the title "When Will It Be?", the editorialists at the *Globe and Mail* ("Canada's National Newspaper") meditated on the temporality of the news in a confessional mode uncharacteristic of daily journalism in language worth citing at some length:

> Tell us you couldn't see this coming and we will not believe you. Michael Jackson, the bleached and rhino-plasticated pop star and his wife, Lisa Marie Presley, the heir of another great musician consumed by his greatness, have decided to call it quits. This comes as little surprise to anyone. . . . There was never a question of whether. The only news was when.
>
> Which is the case with more news than we'd normally care to admit. Take sports: Two teams will play at stuffing a ball in a hoop or

> swatting it across a net or clubbing it over a fence and, sure as Cher is to continue to appear on awards shows as a parody of haute couture, one team will win and another will lose. And we will keep watching, because in a world of transcendent unknowns, comfort and the illusion of control come from seeing unpredictability chained, transformed into an event where chance is channeled and hemmed in, its ultimate destination never in doubt. The when, how and why can be subject to endless permutations, but the what is never at issue.
>
> That Canada will be hit by winter storms in the winter and scorched by summer heat in the summer is predictable, and when it happens, it is news. Tides are drawn by the moon, rivers swell with spring runoff, active volcanoes explode and the earth quakes on well-publicized fault lines, and it is news. Nostradamus spoke of things that will come to pass, but he never told us when. . . .
>
> Indeed, the culminating event of human existence falls within this genus of news. One of the world's great newspapers, The Times of London, made a name for itself on this sort of coverage. A small staff prepared stories on news that had yet to happen, yet which every editor could say without the slightest doubt or hesitation surely would. Those scribes were blessed with no great power of divination, they were merely realists, and it is in this spirit of realism that they prepared that news staple, obituaries of the great, filing them in anticipation of the appropriate day. Death is news, and death is only a matter of when. (D6)

It would seem that a newspaper can make a name for itself—such a name as the *Times*, for example—through the exercise of a realism that transcribes the news in advance of its occurrence, transforming unpredictability into a certain event, to include "the culminating event of human existence," which is "never a question of whether," but "only a matter of when." Indeed, death exemplifies this genus of news and its reporting before the fact this spirit of realism.

A specific instance of that spirit at work in the pages of the venerable London daily is readable in the issue published on February 21, 1994. Two ostensibly distinct articles that shared the front page (separated by an update on the siege of Sarajevo by the Bosnian Serb army) prove upon closer scrutiny to be intimately linked—indeed, versions of a story arguably one and the same. Above the fold, the *Times* reported on the vote, expected in the House of

Commons later in the day, on a bill proposing the reduction of the homosexual age of consent from twenty-one to sixteen. The article's author, Jonathan Prinn, judged that "The result is too close to call, with any of the three main options—reducing the age of consent to 16, reducing it to 18 and leaving it at 21—remaining possible outcomes" ("Gay Age of Consent," 1). Below the fold appeared a photographic portrait of Derek Jarman with an announcement of his recent death "after a long battle against Aids."

Those with the time to read further might have been struck by the thoroughgoing realism that informed reporting and editorializing on the age-of-consent debate as well as Jarman's death and by the repressed but still legible links between the two events. If the author of the front-page report characterized the prospective vote as "in the balance" at the time he filed his story, the relative anonymity of the editorial page allowed the weight of a realist ideology to tip the scales. Beneath the newspaper's logo, which features the image of a clock presiding over the publication's title (the name it has made for itself) inscribed as if on the pages of an open book, flanked by other volumes bearing the imprints "Times Past" and "The Future," ran a lengthy column entitled "Voting for Change":

> Today the House of Commons will decide whether to lower the age of consent for homosexual men. . . .
>
> The cultural impact of such a change is naturally hard to predict. . . .
>
> This debate has raised fundamental questions about the relationship between law and morality. To some extent, the champions of 16 have argued against themselves. Changes in social attitudes have indeed made reform desirable; but social attitudes continue to set the boundaries within which reform must be carried out. Those who are serious about improving the lot of homosexual men must pay careful attention to the realities of their own culture. This is why arguments about the age of consent in other countries are beside the point. . . . It is the likely response of Britons to a prospective change in the law that MPs must judge when they choose between 16, 18 and 21. . . .
>
> Law can have an educational effect, ushering a community towards greater tolerance. What it cannot do is impose abstract moral propo-

> sitions suddenly upon a mass of people. Legislation is a more complex business than philosophical debate; liberties are better grounded in consensus than diktat. To vote for 18 is to choose a middle course. But, as Edmund Burke warned the Sheriffs of Bristol, moderation is not always 'a sort of treason.' (15)

Among the "champions of 16" who consistently transgressed the boundaries set by moderation and the middle course was the filmmaker, painter, and author whose obituary appeared in full two pages later in the same edition: "Derek Jarman was the first to acknowledge the dark irony that wide public recognition of his achievements in British cinema only followed disclosure in 1987 that he was suffering from the Aids virus. It demonstrated, he said, a 'vulture culture'" (17). The irony cited here darkens further in light of the conjunction of events made explicit in a very different obituary account, that of AIDS activist Simon Watney:

> In 1991 [Jarman] had said, 'I want to be a part of the final alteration in the laws on homosexuality and I want to tend my garden.' In early February this year he made the decision to come off all his medical treatments; at the time, the House of Commons was preparing to vote on a bill proposing a lowering of the age of consent for gay men, from 21 to 16. Jarman campaigned passionately for this bill, and had said that he was living on only to see it passed. On the morning of February 21, however, *The Times* and other newspapers were put in the position of carrying front-page stories about both the age-of-consent vote, to take place later that day, and Derek's death. In the event, a dishonorable compromise—a lowering to 18 instead of 16—was passed. The U.S. has already witnessed the extraordinary symbolism of 'political funerals,' in which the ashes of people with AIDS are thrown onto the lawns of the White House, at their request, to protest ongoing government neglect. Derek's was a self-consciously political death. ("Derek Jarman," 119)[1]

The "self-consciously political" aspect of the death at hand was evidently lost on the obituarists at the *Times*, who (writing, perhaps, before the event) settled for a predictable enumeration of Jarman's "achievements in British cinema" and a low-risk wager on his legacy:

"One year earlier, during British Film Year, Jarman had railed against the exclusion of independent film-makers, like himself, from the trumpeted parade of British glories. But time will ensure his place in history, as a proud, passionate artist of singular gifts" (17).

No reader of Jarman's oeuvre can rest in peace with such an account of his life and death, particularly in the context of the editorial-page admonition, cited earlier, that "Those who are serious about improving the lot of homosexual men must pay careful attention to *the realities of their own culture*" (emphasis added). For Jarman's multifaceted corpus tirelessly contests the ownership of the culture in question, just as it resists precisely the sort of realism he associated with the "vulture culture" of a certain journalism and its readership. That resistance finds specific form in what he termed "dream allegory" (*Last of England*, 188), deployed in many of his films and paintings as well as in a copious body of written work that includes the journals he kept in 1989–90, published under the title *Modern Nature*. The form and force of that allegory yield a sense of time, place, and history utterly removed from that so blithely invoked by the realist scribes at the *Times*.

~

to whom it may concern
in the dead stones of a planet
no longer remembered as earth
may he decipher this opaque hieroglyph
perform an archeology of soul
on these precious fragments
all that remain of our vanished days

—Derek Jarman, *Modern Nature*

The pages of *Modern Nature* are in part a gardener's diary of planting and tending, and as such they regularly include reports of the weather that traverses the landscape at Dungeness, the seaside location of Jarman's home, Prospect Cottage, and its adjoining garden.[2] A number of commentators—including Jarman's lover Keith Collins, the "HB" of the journals and the garden's caretaker since the filmmaker's death—have noted the obviously allegorical dimensions of a garden that thrives against the odds in the long shadow of the Dungeness B nuclear power plant while its gardener fights to forestall the opportunistic infections that batter an immune system weakened by HIV.[3] (The garden is thus among the "Landscapes of time, place, memory, imagined landscapes" to which he alludes in a subsequent memoir entitled *At Your Own Risk* [3].) Of the elements Jarman so frequently invokes, none is more telling than the wind, whose movements and effects he records at greatest length in the entry for February 24, 1989, which begins with mundane notations (what he elsewhere in the journal terms "everyday jottings" [*Modern Nature*, 207]) about the conditions under which he writes: "A grey windy day, cold too. The winter we nearly forgot arrived last night and is set to circle around us for a few days. I placed driftwood in front of the house to mark a new bed—but decided to leave the digging for a warmer day" (*Modern Nature*, 18). Constraints placed on the day's gardening afford an occasion for memory work, commencing with the recollection of another windy day and its effects on a younger Jarman: "As the black twister hurled the little house in Kansas through the raging clouds to Oz, I bolted through the cinema and out into the street. How often in my childhood dreams have I found myself trapped on the emerald floors, pursued by the armies of the Wicked Witch" (*Modern Nature*, 18). The memory of an early cinematic experience, rehearsed in subsequent dreams, yields a generalization—"Childhood memories have a funny habit of repeating themselves"—that in turn opens onto the recollection of more recent meteorological terror: "On the now famous October night of the Great Storm about a year ago, I awoke in the early hours of morning from a fitful sleep. A sharp wind had sprung up. At first I thought little of it; Dungeness is known to be exposed and the wind blows here without ceasing" (*Modern Nature*, 18). In fact, Jarman wrote his entry only a few months after the October storm: The unsettling memory of the wind seems here to disorient his sense of time.[4] He goes on to recount in detail his experience of the violent effects of an invisible force:

> The first dull waves of panic washed over me. I dressed fumbling in the dark. Feeling cold and nauseous I groped my way by the spectral

> beam of the lighthouse towards the kitchen at the back of the house, which was taking the full brunt of a storm increasing its intensity by the minute. I found a candle and lit it; if anything, its guttering flame increased my feelings of insecurity and isolation.
>
> Outside the nuclear power station glowed in the dark. I blew out the candle. A fisherman's hut disintegrating seemed in the dark to be the house itself; every timber was stretched to the breaking point. Now and again a board split from its neighbor, 80 years of tar and paint parting like a rifle shot. The house was breaking up. I sat and waited for the roof to blow away or a window to cave in.
>
> The hurricane grew. A deep and continuous roar now underpinned the higher notes of gutter and drainpipe: the shrieks and groans and banshee whistling took on symphonic proportion. My Prospect Cottage never seemed so dear, beaten like a drum in the rushing wind that assaulted it and flew on howling after other prey. Down the coast whole roofs of tiles were lifted high in the air, to descend in a ceramic hail. A garden wall collapsed in a series of curves like a serpent, an ancient macrocarpa shredded like matchsticks. Outhouses groaned and slid off their foundations. (*Modern Nature*, 19)

In time the storm subsides, and Jarman's fear for the fate of his beloved cottage is allayed in terms that draw on his earlier recollection of the more notorious twister:[5] "Yet Prospect stood firm on its foundations, unlike the farm in Kansas. Without light or heat for the next week, I stared at the glittering power plant on the horizon and wondered if, like the Emerald City and the great Oz himself, my life and this cottage had been dreamt all those years ago in Rome" (*Modern Nature*, 19).

The childhood sojourn in Italy, here aligned with Dorothy's Kansas, is evoked several pages earlier in the journal in the entry for February 13, which begins (again typically) with his account of the damage lately inflicted on his rosemary, crocus, and daffodils by the unrelenting Dungeness winds.[6] He there recalls living with his family in the Borghese Gardens, the remains of the villa built by Scipione Borghese early in the seventeenth century, "in a flat requisitioned from Admiral Ciano, the uncle of Mussolini's foreign secretary" (*Modern Nature*, 14). Jarman's fond reminiscence of riding a donkey "through glades of acanthus, under old cedar trees to a water clock which kept time on a cascade of fern covered rocks" prompts a rumination on temporality and history as figured in the ruined Roman paradise:

> Time itself must have started in earnest after the Fall, because the seven days in which the world was created we now know was an eternity. The ancient Egyptians, whose lives were measured by the annual rise and fall of the Nile, were amongst the first to mark its passage systematically; the Borghese garden commemorates the Egyptians with a gateway in the form of twin pylons. (*Modern Nature*, 14)

The passage posits for "Time itself" a postlapsarian scene of origins, such that temporality bears from the outset the stamp of a knowledge that will seek to master time, to measure and keep it, and eventually to supply its historiography:

> In every corner the park mapped out Time's History: its glades were strewn with monuments to mark its passing. Not the least of which was a circle of marble worthies put up at the end of the nineteenth century to celebrate the unification of Italy: a series of pasty po-faced poets, politicians, musicians and engineers, who had paved the way for the modern state. . . .
>
> What Scipione with his grand vision would have thought of all these worthies in the ruins of his Eden I cannot imagine. He strutted about in his cardinal's scarlet and built a dynasty and his ostentatious polychrome villa: a vulgar gilded pleasure palace in the modern manner, filled with yet more antique marbles. A far cry from Adam's wooden hut in Paradise, no doubt built from the timbers of the tree of knowledge—the very first house. . . .
>
> One day I returned home to our flat in via Paesiello for tea, to find that the seven days of the week were now mapped out by bells—and lessons at the American School.
>
> Years later, in 1972, I returned to the Borghese gardens with a soldier I met in the Cinema Olympia. He had thrown his arms around me in the gods; later we made love under the stars of my Eden. (*Modern Nature*, 14)

The vulgar monumentality enlisted in the consolidation of the modern Italian state stands in sharp contrast to the dream allegory whose foundations are laid in this recollection. With his belated return to the gardens in the company of his lover, Jarman in effect regains the paradise ("my Eden") lost to Adam. As he writes in *At Your Own Risk*,

> An orgasm joins you to the past. Its timelessness becomes the brotherhood; the brethren are lovers; they extend the 'family.' I share that sexuality. It was then, is now and will be in the future. . . .
>
> There was a night when I clicked into the ghost of one of my heroes, Caravaggio. It was an odd moment in which the past actually flashed into the present, physically—fucking with the past if you like. (31)

The "timelessness" he here ascribes to his sexuality—"a far cry" from "time with beginning and end, literal time, monotheist time, for which you are unfailingly charged" (*Modern Nature*, 30)—serves as something of a shorthand for the temporality of dream allegory, in which "the poet wakes in a visionary landscape where he encounters personifications of psychic states. Through these encounters he is healed. . . . Here [the specific reference is to his film *The Last of England*] the present dreams the past future. . . . Its structure suggests a journey: pages turn in a book bringing with them new turnings in direction, building up an atmosphere without entering into traditional narrative" (*Last of England*, 188). It is also, in *Modern Nature*, the time to which the gardener lays claim: "The gardener digs in another time, without past or future, beginning or end. A time that does not cleave the day with rush hours, lunch breaks, the last bus home. As you walk into the garden you pass into this time—the moment of entering can never be remembered. Around you the landscape lies transfigured. Here is the Amen beyond the prayer" (30). In these terms, his present life, his beloved cottage and garden at Dungeness, are the allegorical "transfiguration" of the Roman remains, as Oz is the transfiguration of Kansas. The "Winds of Change" have transformed the black and white of the past, whirling them up in a vortex that transplants the very horizon (*Last of England*, 179).

Still, Jarman does not yet dwell over the rainbow. And as the diary entry for February 24 unfolds, it becomes clear that its stakes are not solely autobiographical, not limited to the promise of his own future made good in the fabled pot of gold. Rather, the journal elaborates a prophetic dream of historical dimensions. Following an account of the end of the October storm, the entry proceeds to trace the movements of another wind, figurative of still other forces:

> I live in borrowed time, therefore I see no reason in the world why my heart grows not dark.
>
> A cold wind blows tonight over this desolate island.
>
> Over the hills and dales, over mountain and marsh, down the great roads and little lanes, through the villages and small towns, through the great towns and the cities.
>
> Everywhere it blows through empty streets and desolate houses, rattling the hedgerows and broken windows, drumming on locked doors.
>
> The wind is blowing high in the tower blocks and steeples, down along the river, invading houses and mansions, through the corridors and up the staircases, rustling the faded curtains in bedrooms, over the carpets, up the aisles and down in the crypts, in public places and private, among forgotten secrets, round the armchair, the easy chair, across the kitchen table.
>
> So icy is this wind that it rattles the bones in the graves and sends rats shivering down the sewers.
>
> Fragments of memory eddy past and are lost in the dark. In the gusts yellowing half-forgotten papers whirl old headlines up and over the dingy suburban houses, past leaders and obituaries, the debris of inaction, into the void. Thought illuminated briefly by lightning. The rainbows are put out, the crocks of gold lie rusting—forgotten as the fallen trees which strew the fields and dead meadows. (*Modern Nature*, 20)

Max Horkheimer's televised experiment with reading out-of-date newspapers, which served as a reference point in Part II, above, is here radicalized, its mise-en-scène spun out of control by an incalculable force at work.[7] Old headlines and obituaries are cast as "the debris of inaction," of moderation and the middle course, the betrayal of the rainbow's promise.[8] In this scenario, which again alludes to the passage from Kansas to Oz, the "rather gray papers" of Horkheimer's armchair exercise reappear in color, as testament to what Jarman elsewhere calls "The Perils of Yellow": "It's a hundred years since the Yellow Press invented itself in New York; warmongering and xenophobic, it fights for the yellow in your pocket. Cultural cuckold. Raving, betraying, mental" (89).[9]

Indeed, "yellowing half-forgotten papers" figure as the moldering remnants of thoughtlessness and compromise throughout Jarman's corpus. In the overt allegory of his film *The Last of England*, for example, the "royal baby" appears crying inconsolably, swaddled in an issue of the *Sun* whose headline announces the outbreak of the Falklands War ("War with the Argies Only Hours Away"). And a series of paintings exhibited in 1992 under the title *Queer* enlists "the accumulated anti-gay front pages of the yellow press" (166) in canvases including "Sick," "Blood," "Spread the Plague," "Dead Angels" and "Letter to the Minister."[10] In *Modern Nature*, the artist plots a forthcoming installation in Glasgow:

> Spent the morning rewriting *Blueprint* and afterwards caught the 24 up to Albert Road to see Simon Watney, who has the most complete archive of media disinformation. I have decided to dedicate each of the tarred and feathered beds to a newspaper, *Mirror*, *Star*, *Sun*, *Guardian*, *Times*, they've stolen the best of names and all of them have put out dangerous and false information. . . .
>
> Quotations from the newspapers, photos of loved ones and families, found photos, alarm clocks, a telephone, a tarred and feathered TV.
>
> In the centre of the gallery an oasis: a bed with two young men surrounded by barbed wire; press cuttings, as if blown by the wind. . . . (126–27)

It is in his autobiographical writings that Jarman's contempt for yellow journalism—a "virus" against which he opposes the "cultural condom" of Plato's *Symposium* and Shakespeare's sonnets—gathers full force (*Modern Nature*, 163–64). *Modern Nature* provides several instances of the tabloids' targeting of his own life and work: "The *People* has a lurid article: *Movie Boss with AIDS—Glad to die in a shack*! What people do to sell newspapers! I don't know how they can live with their consciences—though of course, out of use so long, they have shrivelled to the size of an appendix" (75). Or again: "In one of his newspapers Mr. Maxwell, retired chairman of the National AIDS Foundation, headlined me today as 'AIDS victim to stage Pets.' I mistakenly thought the *Mirror* a little more responsible than the *People*, but fact and truthful reporting are always the victims of money" (85).[11] One of the most savage entries in the journal, dated June 11, 1989, transcribes Jarman's staging of an encounter with one yellow journalist:

> A letter from the *Folkestone Herald* alerted me: the *Sun* wanted to buy their photos of me. Meanwhile the lawyers' letters to the *People* and the *Mirror* have produced an apology and a correct reporting of my HIV status under the headline 'Del's Not Dying.'
>
> A motorbike draws up and a hapless reporter from the *Sun* clambers off. This is his third trip down here from London.
>
> 'Do you mind if I photo you?'
>
> 'Yes, but since one way or another you're going to, we might as well do a good job of it. Not in front of the house, on the beach.'
>
> We trek off across the shingle. I sense he wants to get this assignment over with as quickly as possible. I offer to carry his camera bag with a malicious smile. When we set up at the water's edge he says,
>
> 'I'm only a snapper.'
>
> 'Well,' I say, 'this is your chance to take a decent photo.' I fix him with a basilisk stare as he clicks away.
>
> 'You look uncomfortable,' he remarks.
>
> 'Not as much as *you* should.'
>
> 'Oh?'
>
> 'I'm writing a diary, which I'm publishing. You're today's entry. When all is said and done what I choose to write will, I expect, be the only trace of your life. Your memory is in my hands.'
>
> Long silence.
>
> 'The *Sun*'s not kept by the British Museum, the paper destroys itself, it's so acid. When you get back tell your editor to read the retraction in the *People*. Because next time I'm going for a million unless it's right. Mr. Maxwell, the retired captain of the AIDS Foundation, has seen better to print an apology.'
>
> I kept him snapping for as long as I could. I hope he remembers the session. (*Modern Nature*, 94–95)

Beyond the threat of a certain revenge ("Your memory is in my hands"), what takes place in this exchange is a specific linguistic event, a prophetic wager on Jarman's part. Given newsprint's material vulnerability, its predictable self-destruction over time (as yellowing yields to disintegration), he calculates that "when all is said and done" the only trace of the reporter's life that will survive this biodegradation will be what Jarman deigns to record in "today's entry" in his journal. In a sense, he scripts the unwitting reporter's obituary before the fact, laying odds on his interlocutor's future as the *Times*'s obituarists will lay odds on his own (and exacting in advance an oblique revenge on the realist scribes themselves).[12]

Of course, readable throughout Jarman's work is a keen and consistent awareness of the ephemerality not only of the hated "debris of inaction" but of his own production, likewise destined to pass away. In one of many acknowledgements of this fact in *Modern Nature*, Jarman cites the biblical Book of Wisdom, 2:4–5:

> Our name will be forgotten in time
> And no one will remember our works
> Our life will pass away like the traces of a cloud
> And be scattered like mist
> That is chased by the rays of the sun
> And overcome by its heat
> For our allotted time is the passing of a shadow
> And will run like sparks through the stubble
> (109; cf. *Chroma*, 124)

As Derrida remarks in a diary fragment of his own, circulated under the title "Biodegradables" and cited in the introduction, above, this is the double bind in which the published text, in whatever medium, always finds itself: "As biodegradable, it is on the side of life, assimilated . . . by a culture that it nourishes, enriches, irrigates, even fecundates, but on the condition that it lose its identity, its figure, or its singular signature, its proper name" (824). His analysis of the translatability to culture of the figure of the "biodegradable" articulates a dual necessity:

> In the most general and novel sense of this term, a *text* must be '(bio)degradable' in order to nourish the 'living' culture, memory, tradition. To the extent to which it has some sense, makes sense, then its 'content' irrigates the milieu of this tradition and its 'formal' identity is dissolved. . . . And yet, to enrich the 'organic' soil of the said culture, it must also resist it, contest it, question and criticize it enough . . . and thus it must not be assimilable ([bio]degradable, if you like). Or at least, it must be assimilated as inassimilable, kept in reserve, unforgettable because irreceivable, capable of inducing meaning without being exhausted by meaning, incomprehensibly elliptical, secret. (845)

It is perhaps the horticulturist in Jarman that disposes him to reflect on the equivocal fate of his own work in terms of its eventual biodegradation. In *The Last of England*, for example, he writes that he "could never quite understand the '60's painters who wanted their paintings to fall to pieces, it wasn't as if the 500 years they could have lasted was very long. *Everything falls to the ground like dead leaves*, making a rich compost, Greek statues are pulverized for lime, Roman wall paintings decay and fertilize, others grow out of them" (40, emphasis added). "Like dead leaves," his own films, paintings and writings are so much windfall destined to fertilize the future.

Once again, the wind inscribes itself as a force to be reckoned with. As Jarman translates it elsewhere in *Modern Nature*: "Quid sit futurum cras fuge quaerere et quem fors dierum cinque dabit lucro appone, nec dulcis amores. . . . Try not to guess what lies in the future, but as fortune deals days enter them into your life's book as windfalls" (106). His free rendering of the unattributed citation in effect figures the journal entries themselves—collectively, Jarman's "life's book"—as windfalls: material evidence of a force that circulates invisibly. (He writes in *Chroma* that "My pen chased this story [of friends dead or dying] across the page tossed this way and that in the storm" [110].) As force, it is strictly irreducible to meaning and hence itself resistant to decay and disintegration:

> What resists immediate degradation is this very thing . . . which is no longer on the order of meaning and which joins the universal wealth

> of the 'message' to unintelligible singularity, finally unreadable (if reading means to understand and to learn to know), of a trace or a signature. . . . The 'proper name' in question—which has no meaning and is not a concept . . . is proper to nothing and to no one, reappropriable by nothing and by no one, not even by the presumed bearer. It is this singular impropriety that permits it to resist degradation—never forever, but for a long time. (Derrida, "Biodegradables," 845)

If they are not to remain utterly unintelligible, such forces, however irreducible to sense and resistant to degradation, cannot forego entirely a certain domesticating figuration. Hence the allegorical formalization of the wind recurs in *Modern Nature*, in contexts ranging from classical mythology to contemporary popular culture.[13] But Jarman is particularly struck by the attempts of two fellow artists—one a painter, the other a filmmaker—to capture the wind in their respective media.

In a pair of successive journal entries, Jarman muses at some length on the painting of Anselm Kiefer, with whom he feels an aesthetic "kinship" based on the German artist's rendering of "frozen, inert burials, firestorms, cinders, great leaden tomes, spidery nervous wires, odd submarine encrustations, amphora from the wrecks of memory, monumental ruins beached between the Tigris and Euphrates . . . the 20th century ashes" (*Modern Nature*, 131). He recounts a recent visit to the "awe-inspiring" exhibition in a London gallery:

> At the Kiefer show a little boy, in long white shorts and a white shirt, perfectly silent in the vast space, stared along the railway lines in a painting, captured a dandelion seed that blew across the floor. He performed a strange dance with it, leaping into the air, crawling about catching it. No-one except an old lady noticed, and she smiled with me. The painting of the tulips has just such movements (coup de vent), the petals blow in the air. How do you paint the wind? This is how. The little boy could have leapt from the paintings. (*Modern Nature*, 132)

The wind—like "Time itself"—can only be figured metonymically, in its effects: as windfall (dandelion seed, tulip petal) in both its senses, as the material trace of the wind's passing, and, as the *Oxford English Dictionary* has it, as "a sudden or unexpected acquisition or advantage."

The second attempt is "a ravishing film by Joris Ivens, at 90 chasing the elusive wind in China" (*Modern Nature*, 175).[14] This "perfect film of the wind" (*Modern Nature*, 281) haunts the Jarman of the journals, even in the dark days of his illness. The diary entry for May 27, 1990, begins at Prospect Cottage: "Night sweat, hair sopping wet and freezing in the small hours. I have no strength at all. I tried to dig up a dead plant and collapsed. I can just walk to the end of the garden. . . . I'm as breathless as an octogenarian" (*Modern Nature*, 290). He resumes writing later in the day, from his hospital bed ("Almoth Wright ward"):

> Joris Ivens walking breathless into the desert to find the wind. Asthmatic. My childhood asthma takes me to the seaside, Bexhill, with Grandma Moselle. Breathless in the hotel.
>
> Now I cannot move. If I do I'm overwhelmed with coughing, my breath stops up, panic. Pneumonia plays its own pipes that wheeze and grumble. Simon Watney says it's an 'after tremor.' What more do I need? Pneumonia and TB. Will I stand up to this?
>
> The shadowy black bats of breathlessness swarm through the evening, roost in my lungs. The oxygen whistles up my nose like water gurgling at a dentist's. There's nothing quite as frightening as losing your breath in an attack of coughing. Clasped by the velvet wings of the bats, I throw the sheets back. At the end of the film Joris found the wind in the desert. Septrin drips into my arm, blood taken from the arteries stings like a bee. Pneumocystis—till they learnt you die from this. I would mercifully pass from asphyxia to unconsciousness. (290–91)

Intricated in Jarman's account are Ivens' "breathless" search for the wind in the desert, memories of his own childhood asthma, and the pneumonia and tuberculosis that threaten him with asphyxia even as he writes. If his chief concern earlier in the journal was with the wind's effects on the Dungeness landscape, it is now, of necessity, rather with internal weather (after all, as he writes in *Chroma*, "What need of so much news from abroad when all that concerns either life or death is transacting and at work within me?" [107]). As his health declines, he is left increasingly "winded": "The cold continues, the frozen larks creep about. I catch my breath. As the light fades, death comes" (*Modern Nature*, 51); "A disturbed day after a week on the run. The silence has left me winded" (117); "I walked dazed through the debris, before I called up a second wind" (157); "By midnight my bronchial chest had winded me. I returned to bed breathless" (223); "A little death overtakes me as I reel breathless into the final [underground] carriage" (226); "I'm rediscovering breathing. I'm up, and off the oxygen, though still breathless" (293); "Breathless in the wind, picked white stones" (301).

As the wind's violent battering of his house and garden formerly unsettled him, and in particular disoriented his sense of time, the breathlessness brought on by his illness does likewise. The journal's record of one lengthy hospital stay bears no dates; its entries are marked only with the days of the week: "Wednesday. I am out of synch. I had a terrible shock this morning when I discovered that I had muddled the days so much that I missed my scan. . . . (this happened today . . . no, I think yesterday . . . no, it's today). . . . I'm so confused by what has happened that I've forgotten whether it was today or yesterday. But in fact it was today. I'm suffering from a confusion in time" (270–71); "Tuesday . . . it's only now I realise what a delirium I have been in for the last five weeks, no sense of time. This diary gives the wrong impression, it's much too focused. I'm emerging from a strange dream. Today time seems to have some measure of form" (274–75).

But again, though the unforgiving wind leaves its traces on him, its movement is never reducible to the rhythms of breath, nor its allegorical force to autobiographical sense. In the pivotal entry (February 24, 1989) that recalls the October storm, as elsewhere, the narrative of its activity retains the contours of a prophetic dream:

> But the wind does not stop for my thoughts. It whips across the flooded gravel pits drumming up waves on their waters that glint hard and metallic in the night, over the shingle, rustling the dead gorse and skeletal bugloss, running in rivulets through the parched grass—while

I sit here in the dark holding a candle that throws my divided shadow across the room, and gathers my thoughts to the flame like moths.

I have not moved for many hours. Years, a lifetime, eddy past: one, two, three: into the small hours, the clock chimes. The wind is singing now.

Eternity, eternity
Where will you spend eternity?
Heaven or hell, which shall it be?
Where will you spend eternity?

And then the wind is gone, chasing itself across the shingle to lose itself in the waves which brush past the Ness, throwing up plumes of salt spray which spatter across the windows. Nothing can hide from it. Certainly no man can be wise before he has lived his share of winters in the world.

The wind calls my name, Prophesy.

Long past the creator destroyed this earth, the joyful songs of the people were silent, the ancient works of giants stood desolate.

The wind whirls in the gutters, screams in the telegraph poles.

I'll huff and I'll puff,
And I'll blow your house down.

Time is scattered, the past and the future, the future past and present. Whole lives are erased from the book by the great dictator, the screech of the pen across the page, your name, Prophesy, your name! The wind circles the empty hearth casting a pall of dust, the candle fizzes. Who called this up? Did I?

Now throughout the world stand windblown halls, frost-covered ruined buildings; the winehalls crumble, kings lie dead, deprived of pleasure, all the steadfast band dead by the wall. (*Modern Nature*, 20–21)

This, then, may count as Jarman's own attempt to capture the wind in the third medium in which he labors. The language in this passage is not limited to a descriptive function; rather, it personifies the wind, figuratively conferring upon it a voice that sings, screams, and "calls my name, Prophesy." In what follows, "my name" becomes "your name, Prophesy, your name!"—and the question of who is addressing whom remains suspended. To recall Derrida's formulation, "The 'proper' name in question—which has no meaning and is not a concept. . . . is proper to nothing and to no one, reappropriable by nothing and by no one, not even by the presumed bearer. It is this singular impropriety that permits it to resist degradation—never forever, but for a long time" ("Biodegradables," 845).

What Jarman's text and the wind may be said to share is a force of singular impropriety, a force that prophesies past, present and future resistance to any easy determination of sense, any ready assimilation to understanding. In *Modern Nature*, as in Jarman's mature work more generally, the force of dream allegory eludes recuperation by a realism that would dictate (in advance and among other things) that "death is only a matter of when." For this corpus is the testament of a survivor:

> Shall I begin on the day that I was overwhelmed by guilt? I had survived. . . . As the years passed, I saw in the questioner's eyes the frustrations of coming to terms with life; are you still here? Some were brutally frank: 'When are you going to die?'
>
> Didn't you know I died years ago with David and Terry, Howard, the two Pauls. This is my ghostly presence, my ghostly eye. 'I had AIDS last year,' I said with a smile and they looked at me as if I was treating their tragedy flippantly. 'Oh yes, I had AIDS last year. Have you had it?'
>
> *Now it doesn't matter when I die, for I have survived. . . .*
>
> It's been five years now and I still return to the ABC of HIV. Talk of condoms, safe, safer, safest sex again and again. The papers act delinquent, put the clock back to sell a fear, if you open up to them sure enough, they'll shoot you down. Well, we knew that would happen. (*At Your Own Risk*, 10, emphasis added)

That was only a matter of when.

Reference Matter

Notes

Chapter 1

1. The transcript of the hearing before the House Subcommittee on International Operations reads as follows:

Mr. Mica [Chair]: Mr. Dertadian, with regard to an option, we're going to introduce a new word that I learned in Moscow, to potentially deconstruct a portion of a building. Deconstruct the top two floors. How much does it cost to deconstruct a building, one or two floors?

Mr. Dertadian: We're looking at various options, depending on what the option is decided on, and we are looking at options of deconstructing and demolishing, whatever the word is. It depends on how you are going to do this.

Mr. Mica: Is it feasible that to deconstruct the top two or three floors of a building of the size that we're talking about it would cost—

Mr. Dertadian: Yes.

Mr. Mica: It is possible, but—

Mr. Dertadian: It is possible.

Mr. Mica: It is possible that it would cost almost as much to reconstruct from the beginning, or no? Is that out of the question?. . . . I have been told that would be enormously expensive to do what this new term now envisions, possibly deconstructing a couple floors, maybe equal, and I may be wrong. That's all I'm asking you. You're the expert. What is the cost of rebuilding the entire building?

Mr. Dertadian: . . . Based on some very preliminary work we've done in looking at options and what they would cost, it would probably cost about as much as we have already spent to deconstruction [sic] and rebuild.

Mr. Mica: So, in other words, we break even by starting over if we did the deconstruct route.

> *Mr. Dertadian*: I don't think we break even, sir. . . . These are very rough figures. (59–60)

Thanks to Thomas Keenan for making available to me both the transcript of the hearings and the *Post* report.

2. For Derrida's account of the way in which the word "deconstruction" initially "imposed itself," see "Deconstruction in America," "Letter to a Japanese Friend," and "Some Statements and Truisms." In the latter, Derrida calls for a vigilant use of quotation marks, "not as a formalist neutralization concerned with propriety but as the reminder of the necessary general contamination, of the transplants and irreducible parasitism which affect any theorem" (78). The term has been appropriated with varying degrees of care (with and without quotation marks) in a wide range of contexts, particularly in cultural reporting. In one notable instance, "deconstruction" has been adopted by the fashion industry to designate a current trend in clothing design practiced by innovative Japanese and Belgian designers including Rei Kawakubo and Martin Margiela.

3. Cf. Paul de Man, writing in 1970 about the impact on literary studies of the new theoretical approaches: "Well-established rules and conventions that governed the discipline of criticism and made it a cornerstone of the intellectual establishment have been so badly tampered with that the entire edifice threatens to collapse" ("Criticism and Crisis," 3).

4. Andrzej Warminski has analyzed the pivotal role played by *Newsweek*'s "A New Look at Lit Crit" in setting this tone. That article's first paragraph is symptomatic: "The study of literature has seldom been as genteel as its subject matter suggests. Teachers of literature are not only scholars but, inherently, critics as well, and they have always fought like intellectual infantry over the interpretations of literary texts. But in recent years the literary scene has dissolved into a state of all-out war" (Woodward et al., "New Look," 80). The cover story in the same issue was, suitably enough, "A Dangerous Nuclear Game," on Israel's bombing of an Iraqi atomic reactor.

5. In "Criticism and Crisis," de Man asks whether "there is not a recurrent epistemological structure that characterizes all statements made in the mood and the rhetoric of crisis" (14). The uniform logic at work in these denunciations of the current state of the humanities suggests that the answer is yes.

6. As Werner Hamacher notes in "Journals, Politics," "Simplifications and their repetitions tend to produce meanings, whether they happen to correspond to the actual texts at hand or not" (447).

7. In a reading of de Man's "The Resistance to Theory," Peggy Kamuf observes that "because the institutionalization of literary theory in this country has tended to follow the way in which it can be made to serve an overarching pedagogical program and because literary theory, when it pursues its main theoretical interest, has to question the defining limits of any such program when applied to literary language, institutionalization can be made to appear in its effects—the marks it has left—on the movement of theoretical thought" ("Pieces of Resistance," 140).

8. This line of argument is indebted to Andrzej Warminski ("Prefatory Postscript," xxxv), who assesses the current critical scene in terms of the hegemony of nonreading and the counterhegemonic, strategic force of reading. See also Godzich, "Culture of Illiteracy," 34.

Chapter 2

1. "De Man treats Husserl with a 'respect' that is more than mere politeness; it acknowledges his own indebtedness, since if he questions Husserl, it is only by extending Husserl's conception of critical self-reflection to the philosopher's determination of self-criticism as 'the historical privilege of European man' (de Man), in order to argue that the very project of attributing universal validity to a localized phenomenon reveals that the notion of self-criticism itself reposes upon an uncriticized, and perhaps uncriticizable, presumption of 'self'" (Weber, "Monument Disfigured," 423, n. 11). We do well to keep in mind such indebtedness when we make use of the critical tools with which de Man has provided us in seeking to dismantle the ideologemes operative in his own early writings.

2. "Derrida, in his recent study of Heidegger, *De l'esprit,* is drawn to cite the same passage. . . . And to the question 'Why recall such a passage and cite it today?' Derrida replies, in part: 'Using the example [*sur l'exemple*] of a discourse that in general is not suspected of [harboring] the worst, it is good to recall that referring to the *spirit,* to *freedom* of the spirit and to the spirit as *European,* could and still can be allied with a politics to which one would like to oppose it.' [Jacques Derrida, *De l'esprit. Heidegger et la question*. Paris: Galilée, 1987, 95 n. 2]" (Weber, "Monument Disfigured," 409).

3. In his reading of Rousseau's *Second Discourse,* de Man allows for such a temporal intervention in what initially appears as a logical contradiction: "Are we forced to conclude that Rousseau's paradoxes are gen-

uine contradictions, that he did not know, in the *Discourse*, what he stated in the *Essay*, and vice versa? Perhaps we should heed his admonition: 'in order not to find me in contradiction with myself, I should be allowed enough time to explain myself'" ("Metaphor (*Second Discourse*)," 149).

4. Higgins examines the "recurrent motif of continuity and rupture" in the efforts in the essays collected in *Responses* to articulate early with late de Man. She also interrogates possible continuities and discontinuities between de Man and deconstruction, collaboration and resistance, journalism and scholarship (Review, 108–9).

5. On the constitutive blindness of philosophical reflection, see also Slavoj Žižek: "There is the theatre in which your truth was performed before you took cognizance of it. The confrontation with this place is unbearable because philosophy as such *is defined* by its blindness to this place" (*Sublime Object*, 19–20).

6. The operation of blindness and insight, as de Man understood it, could be summoned as a partial explanation—if one were required—for his disinclination to meet in advance the demand made by John Brenkman and others that he set the record straight with a public confession or apology: "De Man eschewed any acknowledged reflection on his writing and activity during the war. He participated in fascism publicly, but did not abandon it publicly" (Brenkman, "Fascist Commitments," 21)—although, as several essays in *Responses* attest, de Man made his writings for the collaborationist press known to a number of people at critical junctures in his career. Once again, Godzich provides an economical summary: "A blindness constitutive of an insight was far more interesting than the result of its correction would be: at best, the latter would smooth out the argumentative path through which the insight was obtained; at worst, it would erase the traces of the functioning of a cognitive mechanism that forced anyone examining it into wondering about the provenance of insight, and thus of the workings of cognition in general. Correcting errors sets the record straight, eliminates impediments to thought; reflecting upon blindness, on the other hand, forces thought into a reflective judgment about its own tortuous and discontinuous path, the very blindness of which consists in the fact that it has no guide to warn against its vagaries" ("Religion," 155).

7. With reference to de Man's praise of Charles Peguy as a Dreyfusard in the "Chronique littéraire" dated May 6, 1941 ("Notre chronique littéraire," 85–86), Ian Balfour takes note of the effect that the example of Peguy may have exercised on de Man: "By holding up Peguy's life as ex-

emplary, [de Man] offers an implicit contrast to his own position" ("Difficult Reading," 8).

8. The version of the lecture cited here was compiled from three sets of notes recorded by colleagues and students in attendance, including my own. Quotations not otherwise attributed are from this lecture. Taken together, the notes make for a full and detailed, if not verbatim, transcription. De Man's late essays "Phenomenality and Materiality in Kant," "Kant's Materialism," and "Kant and Schiller" are collected in the posthumously published *Aesthetic Ideology*.

9. In his *Life and Works of Goethe*, George Henry Lewes cites the author's reflection on the novel: "In it, as in a burial urn, I have deposited many a sad experience. The 3rd of October 1809 (when the publication was completed) set me free from the work: but the feelings it embodies can never depart from me" (520).

10. Lewes provides an example of the "discussion about the appropriateness" of the interlude, commenting that "A dear friend of mine, whose criticism is always worthy of attention, thinks that the long episodes which interrupt the progress of the story during the interval of Eduard's absence and return, are artistic devices for impressing the reader with a sense of the slow movement of life; and, in truth, it is only in fiction that the denouement usually lies close to the exposition. I give this opinion, for the reader's consideration; but it seems to me more ingenious than just. I must confess that the stress Goethe lays on the improvements of the park, the erection of the moss hut, the restoration of the chapel, the making of new roads, &c., is out of all proportion, and somewhat tedious" (*Life and Works of Goethe*, 525). I am grateful to Lesley Turner for calling this passage to my attention and for noting that the view of Lewes's friend (possibly George Eliot) corresponds to that of de Man in his *Le Soir* review of *The Elective Affinities*.

11. "Nationalism is an agonism. It draws its life not from the natural community of a nation, but from the will to destroy the other, in whose image it is at the same time supposed to be created. The logic of nationalism is the logic of homicidal, suicidal identification" (Hamacher, "Journals, Politics," 439). Hamacher deliberately poses the question: "what was it that *did not prevent* such articles?" For "Only when it is asked in this way is the question not really a question about a hidden determinism to which the intellectuals of that time would have fallen victim; and only when asked in this way does the question give the answer a chance to isolate factors in the situation of intellectuals that would still, *even today*, not

prevent a comparable commitment to a no less disastrous politics" (440). He also reminds us that we should not forget the articles in *Jeudi* that call for a practical critique of the nationalist spirit (439).

12. A "decisive ideological-political point" in such an instance is, in Hamacher's formulation, "to be able, in a given historical moment, to estimate precisely how far the resistance and how far the exploitability of a particular ideologeme reaches" ("Journals, Politics," 444).

13. The model of language as trope was addressed in detail in the lecture preceding this one in the course, given by J. Hillis Miller. See his "A Buchstäbliches Reading": "The basic paradigm of *The Elective Affinities* is the following: Human relations are like the substitutions in metaphorical expressions, or, to put it the other way, since these metaphorical analogies are reversible, the laws of language may be dramatized in human relations" (7).

14. De Man cites the Reichsleiter Baldur von Schirach, who "situates the problem with complete clairvoyance": "'He who calls Goethe a freemason or the "Magic Flute" a freemason opera is not taken seriously by our people. . . . Each great work . . . is always the expression of an isolated personality and, at the same time, of the entire nation. But the nation is not only the current and the immediate, but the eternal community of language and of blood.'" And de Man comments in conclusion, "It is because German literature has conformed to these sage precepts that it has been able to realize its goals and to prepare the way for future greatness" ("Introduction à la littérature," 201).

15. In "Dialogue and Dialogism," de Man interrogates the concept of dialogism as developed in the work of Mikhail Bakhtin.

Chapter 3

1. Lapham borrows his format, with acknowledgement, from Flaubert's *Dictionary of Accepted Ideas.*

2. See also Jane Feuer, "The Concept of Live Television."

3. Perhaps the most successful attempt to take account of the differential specificity of television is that of Samuel Weber in "Television: Set and Screen," 108–28. Weber's deft analysis avoids falling into the twin traps of on the one hand a content analysis that would apply as well to other media, and on the other an ontology that would posit the essence of what is an irreducibly heterogeneous medium. Fredric Jameson distinguishes "three relatively distinct signals" in his valuable analysis of

video, which in his terms functions as mode of aesthetic production, as technology, and as social institution. See his *Postmodernism*, 67.

4. Doane's gloss on Feuer's "The Concept of Live Television" is suggestive for purposes of the present argument: "Although . . . television rarely exploits this technical capability [instantaneous recording, transmission and reception], minimizing not only 'live' transmission but preservation of 'real time' as well, the ideology of 'liveness' works to overcome the excessive fragmentation within television's flow. If television is indeed thought to be inherently 'live,' the impression of a unity of 'real time' is preserved, covering over the extreme discontinuity which is in fact typical of television in the U.S. at this historical moment" (Doane, "Information, Crisis, Catastrophe," 227).

5. Stanley Cavell remarks parenthetically on the way in which "live" television's "point is not to reveal, but to cover (as with a gun), to keep something on view" ("Fact of Television," 252). The analogy between modes of coverage, I would suggest, is not accidental, as the example of the Gulf War makes painfully clear.

6. For example, a *New York Times*/CBS survey on the assassination reported that "Of those polled, 77% said they believed that people besides Lee Harvey Oswald were involved in the killing. And 75% said there was an official coverup in the case" (*New York Times*, February 4, 1992, B1).

7. For an exemplary analysis of these distances, see Weber, "The Media and the War," which appears in the inaugural issue of *Alphabet City*. This issue of the journal provides a range of responses to television's role in the Gulf War. Weber expands on that analysis in "Television: Set and Screen," 108–28. On the ways in which the ideology of "liveness" works to preserve the impression of "real time," see Doane, "Information, Crisis, Catastrophe," 227, and Virilio, *L'écran du desert*, especially 77–82.

8. As Weber notes, "television consists primarily of three operations: *production, transmission* and *reception*. However unified one may take the medium of television to be, it should not be forgotten that the singular noun hides these interrelated but also very different operations, each of which raises a set of very distinct questions and issues" ("Television: Set and Screen," 110).

9. See also Kernan's *The Death of Literature*, especially chapter 6.

10. There is, of course, a substantial and informative body of work in cultural and media studies that has analyzed aspects of television's content and apparatus, but the questions it raises (and sometimes settles) are, with few exceptions, not strictly theoretical.

Chapter 4

1. Statistics on the overwhelming reliance of North Americans on television as their medium of information during the war became available in its immediate aftermath. For example, Scott Williams notes, "While the United States prepared for a ground war against Iraq, a record 81 percent of Americans were getting most of their news from television. . . . And, for the first time, a majority of Americans, 54 percent, mentioned only television as their source of news in February" ("Reliance on TV," C5).

2. See also *Globe and Mail,* February 25, 1991: "Mr. Bush has been reported to have personalized the war in his own mind. His anger at Mr. Hussein is even fiercer than his rage at former Panamanian strongman Manuel Noriega, friends of the President have said. 'If Saddam had just taken the Soviet plan and quietly gone about the business of pulling out,' said one congressional aide over the weekend, 'he might have been able to avoid this. But the kind of florid rhetoric he uses—and I think it's more of a cultural trait than a personal one—drives Bush nuts'" (A11). See also "Gulf War Game Kills Dhaka Boy," *Globe and Mail,* February 25, 1991: "A 12-year-old boy pretending to be George Bush died after being struck by a rock thrown by a playmate who took the role of Saddam Hussein, a Bangladesh newspaper reported Saturday. At least 100 adults were watching the boys, who pretended to be enemies in the Persian Gulf war" (A11).

3. Thomas L. Friedman, "Desert Fog," *New York Times,* February 24, 1991, 4:1. Friedman's article cites Michael J. Sandel, a political theorist at Harvard: "'there is no comparable political clarity about exactly what we want out of this war and what we can expect to achieve. . . . There is still an enormous confusion about our political aims and there is no laser-guided policy to help us. There is no night-vision equipment that can pierce the veils of Middle East politics and define the American role after this war is over'" ("Desert Fog," 4:1).

4. In "Racing Through the Darkness in Pursuit of Scuds," Eric Schmitt writes in the February 24, 1991, edition of the *New York Times*: "'You're trained to hit targets, not people, so you never have to see anyone eye to eye,' said First Lieut. Glenn G. Watson, a 24-year-old weapons officer from Austin, Tex. 'But at night, you sit alone in bed knowing there are people out there and you're bombing them'" (A9).

5. See, for example, the CBS *Evening News,* January 21, 1991, and its broadcast of Defense Department videotape of the smart missile. In fact, the footage was broadcast out of sequence ("We've rolled the wrong tape—

that'll happen sometimes," apologized the aptly named Rather). The network tape temporarily displaced by the military footage was a report by Martha Teischner on the M1A1 tank, "new technology on trial in this war."

6. On the same page as Lorch's article appeared an anonymously authored wire service report that "Iraqis Surrender to Italian TV": "Two groups of Iraqi soldiers have surrendered to an Italian television crew covering the allied ground offensive in Kuwait. The state-run RAI-3 TV showed film today of about a dozen Iraqis walking in the desert toward the television team's camera with their hands up or waving white flags" (A6).

7. I would like to thank Judith Butler and Karin Cope for their insights in our discussions of media coverage of the war as it unfolded.

8. The *Globe and Mail* reported on January 19, 1991, that "Only on the day of President John F. Kennedy's funeral in 1963 was the percentage of American homes tuned into television higher, A. C. Nielsen Co. reported. . . . Because there are many more homes in the U.S. in 1991 than there were in 1963, a greater number of people were watching at 9 PM EST Wednesday, when Bush addressed the nation, than ever before" (3).

9. Doane analyzes this imperative of visibility in televisual discourse in "Information, Crisis, Catastrophe" (226–27). Another of many instances of compliance with this imperative was the NBC *Nightly News* report on the precision of the new bombing technology, in which their military expert put forward an analogy involving a car moving at 55 miles per hour and approaching a vast field from which the driver would be able to pluck a single, targeted blade of grass. Again, the network obliged with footage of a car, a field, and a blade of grass.

10. In this context, see also Richard Dienst's suggestive reworking of Louis Althusser's thesis in the latter's "Ideology and Ideological State Apparatuses." In Dienst's view, Althusser's theory of ideological interpellation "can only be made rigorous by Derrida's postulate of misdirection, which operates at a different level from the Lacanian/Althusserian postulate of misrecognition. At this level, ideology must be conceived as a mass of sendings or a flow of representations whose force consists precisely in the fact that they are not perfectly destined, just as they are not centrally disseminated. Far from always connecting, ideology *never does*: subjects look in on messages as if eavesdropping, as if peeking at someone else's mail" (141). Thomas Keenan provides an incisive commentary on Dienst's argument in "Have You Seen Your World Today?", 104.

11. For a critique of the myth of the so-called couch/war potato, see Constance Penley and Andrew Ross, "Couch Potatoes Aren't Dupes."

Chapter 5

As I was reviewing the edited copy of this manuscript in December 1998, the United States launched another air strike against Iraq. Before the onset of the attack, CNN was once again broadcasting "live" from Baghdad, this time proudly vaunting its innovative "nightscope" technology. Bernard Shaw, anchoring the broadcast, asked the network's military expert about the effect of these luminous images of Baghdad on military planners. "It helps," came the reply, "especially after the fact," in assessing the success of the attack. Antiaircraft fire began a few moments later (CNN broadcast, December 16, 1998).

1. In 1998, Arnett was demoted in the wake of his participation in the controversial broadcast on "Operation Tailwind." Holliman died the same year.

2. During and after the anniversary broadcasts, CNN regularly ran an advertisement that addressed viewers directly, asking "Where were you in Desert Storm?" and culminating with the question, cited as this chapter's epigraph, "Where will you be the next time history happens?"

3. Citations are from CNN transcripts of news reports broadcast on September 3, 1996. At the end of each transcript, a note indicates that "The preceding text has been professionally transcribed. However, although the text has been checked against an audio track, in order to meet rigid distribution and transmission deadlines, it may not have been proofread against tape." The temporal imperatives of the deadline here sanction a certain loss in translation. I am grateful to Thomas Keenan for providing me with the texts.

Chapter 6

1. That it may be "nothing" if it is not a case in point is suggested by the pivotal role of the "O" in the word "Knots" in one version of the series' opening credits, where it is the first letter to appear, a curved line closing in on itself as a figure for the cul-de-sac (Seaview Circle) that serves, particularly in the early seasons, as the locus of action. The O, of course, is likewise readable as the arithmetical zero, a placeholder heterogeneous to the order of number as well as an asemantic cipher. The title of one of the series' episodes, "Will the Circle Be Unbroken," thus poses a question whose answer is clearly negative: The cul-de-sac is always already a broken circle whose inside opens onto an outside that threatens

its integrity *as* inside (reflected in the predictable insider/outsider thematics of the Knots Landing community). This spatialization figures the resistance of the serial format to narrative closure and totalization, as well as the resistance of individual episodes to an unproblematic inscription into an enumerative serial succession. On the frustration of closure in soap opera and melodramatic serial, see, for example, Jeremy Butler, "Notes on the Soap Opera Apparatus," and Sandy Flitterman-Lewis, "All's Well that Doesn't End."

2. Susan Littwin writes that during the improvisation, which afforded the actors an opportunity to write their own stories, "Sometimes they were trying to expand their roles; sometimes they were making their characters more likable. But most often they were trying to make their characters more like themselves. What was revealed in the improvisation is the me-and-my-shadow relationship that develops between actor and character on a long-running series. 'I want to do something more with my life,' [Kevin] Dobson tells me on the set one day. 'Do you mean Kevin or Mack [Mackenzie]?' I ask. He shrugs. 'I guess both. They're interchangeable'" ("Flying," 7). Such an identification often takes place on the viewer's side as well, as an effect of the seductively mimetic mode of representation in melodramatic serial television. As if to underscore this presumed interchangeability of roles, when the two episodes were re-run in the summer of 1989, as part of a "Best of *Knots Landing*" sequence, they were preceded by brief scenes in which the actors, out of character, presented themselves as viewers, settling in with popcorn and a box of tissues to watch "Noises Everywhere." This reading seeks to analyze the structures and strategies that may work to disrupt such spectatorial identification (or at least mark the limits of its possibility) and that call for another kind of response.

3. In the 1988–99 season, the venereal disease that plagued the aboriginal community in this account is once again diagnosed in Knots Landing, this time as evidence in the investigation of Valene Ewing's claim that Jill Bennett tried to murder her. Technology, disease, and death are consistently figured as indissociable in the series.

4. Van Wormer's fictive biography of Laura (in *Knots Landing: The Saga of Seaview Circle*, published in 1986, well before any hint of McCashin's departure from the show) relates that "When she was eleven her mother was diagnosed as having brain cancer, and suddenly Laura had a prominent role in the house. She assumed her mother's household duties without complaint. . . . Taking care of her mother gave her a sense of

purpose, of worth, of importance. She was devastated by her mother's death the following year. . . . Her shock turned to grief, then to anger. When left alone with the coffin before the funeral, Laura, with tears running down her face, said, 'I hate you, Mommy, for doing this to me'" (149–50). Van Wormer thus scripts, before the fact, an event in Laura's prehistory to which the episode of her own death allegorically refers.

5. Given the metonymic basis of intimate relations on the cul-de-sac, there is virtually no distinction between neighbors and friends (or enemies). Intersecting with these metonymically constituted relations is a metaphorics of the family, a genealogy predicated on resemblance: of the child to the father, as invoked in Gary's attempt to prove his paternity of Val's twins; of brother to brother, as in Peter Hollister's fraudulent claim to be Sumner's sibling. Sumner's indifference to the "truth" of Peter's claim, his willingness to act as if Peter were his brother and to exploit the relationship regardless of its basis, is characteristic of the "outsider," as Van Wormer designates him (*Knots Landing*, vi).

6. Since there is no material evidence of Laura's death, the possibility of her future return remains open; her final recorded words to her husband are "I'll see you later . . . maybe." As a black-comic counterpoint to the absence of such evidence, part of the action at the wake revolves around an urn on Sumner's coffee table, which turns out to contain the ashes of Peter Hollister (whom the viewer has seen impaled on a spindle and lugged bleeding all over town in the episode in which he dies). The resurrection of the (apparently) dead is, of course, regularly realized in soap operas (e.g., Frisco Jones in *General Hospital*) and in melodramatic serial television (e.g., Bobby Ewing in *Dallas*). Fredric Jameson links this notion of a revocable death to "the decay of plot, for where nothing is irrevocable (in the absence of death in [Walter] Benjamin's sense) there is no story to tell either, there is only a series of experiences of equal weight whose order is indiscriminately reversible" (*Marxism and Form*, 79).

7. Laura's posthumous address to her survivors recalls the audio tape left for Karen by Sid Fairgate, her first husband, who dies on the operating table without having the chance to speak with her one final time, to reassure her face-to-face that "Whatever happens, my love for you will never die."

8. On prosopopoeia as "the fiction of an apostrophe to an absent, deceased, or voiceless entity, which posits the possibility of the latter's reply and confers upon it the power of speech," see de Man, "Autobiography as De-facement," 75–76, 78.

9. This condition is figured, for example, in Laura's requests of and bequests to Karen, whom Laura asks, in the former's capacity as best friend/closest neighbor and exemplary female figure in the community, to act as foster mother to her infant daughter. Her bequest—Karen is free to sell Laura's house to whomever she likes, at any price, to choose, that is, her new next-door neighbor—inscribes the metonymic foundation of cul-de-sac relations in real estate.

10. "However, it's possible that Shackelford, who is very bright and verbal, may feel resigned to things on *Knots Landing.* He thinks that Gary is too weak and self-pitying. 'He ought to get on with his life, become a successful businessman, like his brother [*Dallas*'s J. R. Ewing]. But dramatically that's not going to happen because the show is centered on the women'" (Littwin, "Flying," 10).

11. Cf. Jacqueline Rose, "Jeffrey Masson and Alice James": "If this scenario is important therefore, it is precisely because, as soon as we step past the immediate fact of sexual difference, we find ourselves up against such a blurring of boundaries, of cause and effect . . . a blurring which strikes at the heart of what it means to know a body, to know psychic and sexual distinction, to know the very limit of the real" (191).

12. In this connection, see also John Wyver, "Television and Postmodernism."

13. Mack, who until his resignation worked as a special prosecutor for the governor of California, kept a framed eight-by-ten photograph of JFK on prominent display in his office. Ironically, William Devane, who portrayed Greg Sumner on *Knots Landing*, subsequently acted the part of Kennedy in a made-for-TV movie.

14. Of course, this analysis itself runs the risk of appropriating, recuperating the anteriority of the event as knowledge, memory, meaning—or worse, as the pathos of television. But the pathos of this particular televisual discourse cannot long survive the grammar of the serial succession. As Laura's video image inquires of Greg, "So what's next? I mean, what happens now?", the pseudodialogue falters; he is reduced to nodding mute assent, and Laura answers her own question: "Nothing, probably—I know that's what you'd say. You'd say nothing. But I'm not so sure." The answer afforded by the serial format is, of course, "Next week, on *Knots Landing* . . . ," and what transpires in the wake of Laura's death and her haunting apostrophe comes as no surprise: Greg proposes marriage to Laura's longtime rival Abby and uses a prerecorded, self-advertising videotape, on the model of *The Love Connection*, to persuade her to accept.

Chapter 7

1. That the diary's claim on posterity was in Henry James's judgment problematic—given its verbatim transcription, names included, of his own uninhibited bedside gossip—is readable in a suggestion he makes in the same letter: "What I should LIKE to do *en temps et lieu* would be should no catastrophe meanwhile occur—or even if it should!—to edit the volume with a few eliminations of text and dissimulations of names, give it to the world and then carefully burn with fire our own four copies"—the copies provided to the surviving brothers by Alice James's companion Katherine Loring (*Diary*, 20).

2. Mary Jacobus notes that Alice James displaces onto "the shape of the British doctor" the symptoms of hysteria: "the spectacle of impotent paralysis that he presents is truly pitiful" (*Diary*, 225; cited in Jacobus, *Reading Woman*, 250). Yeazell's gloss on the mother's diagnosis is instructive as to the applicability but also ultimately the insufficiency of psychoanalytic criticism as an interpretive approach to the diary and the letters: "'Genuine hysteria' verges on an oxymoron, but there seems no reason to doubt the rough accuracy of the diagnosis: all the evidence suggests that Mary James confronted in her daughter as typical a case of that baffling condition as any that were to present themselves to Freud and Breuer some twenty years later in Vienna. From the facial neuralgias and stomach pains to the fainting spells, the mysterious 'attacks' and the partially paralyzed legs, every one of Alice's symptoms was to prove the familiar currency of the *Studies on Hysteria*; like the women whose curious histories would fill that volume, Alice's was a case of physical effects out of all proportion to their apparent causes. . . . But if it is easy enough to imagine Alice's condition become the raw stuff of another case history, to be appended to those of Anna O. and Elisabeth von R., it is virtually impossible to trace the emotional shape such a history would have actually assumed. . . . Observant and acutely intelligent as they could be, the James family were hardly given to the sort of painstaking detective work in which Freud would later engage; when it comes to suggesting the direct causes of Alice's breakdowns, the particular links of emotion and event to which her flesh had thus given expression, the record is generally blank. To guess at the unconscious meanings of Alice's recurrent crises is to beg nearly as many questions as one answers; the private images, the immediate associations of Freud's *Studies* elude us. And . . . it is just such private and seemingly arbitrary connections that always supply the clue" (*Death and Letters*, 11–13).

3. Rose reminds us that in his 1896 Lowell lectures on "Exceptional Mental States," William James defined hysteria as the "hyper-aesthetic disorder." She situates the question of Alice James's hysteria in the context of a reflection on "the question of representation and its limits"; more generally, her claim is that "In relation to psychoanalysis, what seems to have happened is that the terms of the feminist debate have shifted as the question of sexual difference is superseded or absorbed by that of representation (or reveals how the one is implicated in the other), by the loss of innocence—although also of course of guilt—which follows from any troubling of language and the sign" (Rose, "Jeffrey Masson and Alice James," 191–92).

4. Longinus observes in *On the Sublime* that "Tumours are bad things whether in books or bodies, those empty inflations, void of sincerity, as likely as not producing the opposite to the effect intended" (131)—hence Alice James's relief at the physician's damning verdict.

5. Cf. Derrida, *Memoires*, 87n.

6. Cf. de Man, "Promises (*Social Contract*)," 268. I would like to thank Cynthia Chase for her thoughtful commentary on an earlier draft of this essay. Her suggestions helped clarify the stakes of this and other passages.

7. In this way, Sir Andrew's prognosis is comparable to Hyacinth Robinson's paradigmatically indeterminate promise in Henry James's *The Princess Casamassima*. I have analyzed the rhetorical and temporal aspects of this critical speech act in "Promissory Notes: The Prescription of the Future in *The Princess Casamassima*."

8. Published in 1853 in *Putnam's Monthly* magazine; quoted in Jean Strouse, *Alice James*, 45.

9. The performative character of Alice James's relation to death cannot be fully accounted for by a theatrical, a representational model of performance, even though she imagines staging her final scene, "participating in her own death as both audience and leading actress," as Jacobus notes (*Reading Woman*, 250)—as in the passage in which she anticipates (accurately, as it turns out) dying in her sleep, "so that I shall not be one of the audience, dreadful fraud! a creature who has been denied all dramatic episodes might be allowed, I think, to assist at her extinction" (*Diary*, 135; see also 216–17). Crucially, however, as death draws nearer, the pathos of performance in this sense is precluded: "*If it were possible*, with Death so close at hand, to take anything which concerns one's ephemeral personality, with seriousness, I might pose to myself before the footlights

of my last obscure little scene, as a delectably pathetic figure, for I have come to the knowledge within the last week or so that I was simply born a few years too soon . . . "—that is, before the therapeutic possibilities of hypnosis were recognized (*Diary*, 222, emphasis added).

10. As Derrida notes, "Survival isn't simply life after death, but a strange dimension of 'plus de vie'—both 'more life' and 'no more life.' Or 'plus que vie,' that's it, 'more than life.' *Plus de vie* and *plus que vie*" (in Creech, Kamuf, and Todd, "Deconstruction in America, 25).

11. This is Edel's reading, for example (Introduction, 16).

12. On the theoretical consequences of such a thinking of resistance, see Wlad Godzich's "The Tiger on the Paper Mat," xii–xiii; see also Peggy Kamuf: "The concept of resistance has traditionally taken shape along the line of contact between the conceptual faculty and some exteriority. The concept, in other words, shows a double face, turned inward and outward, along the line presumed to divide consciousness from its outside or its other" ("Pieces of Resistance," 141).

13. The quoted letter, of uncertain date, is addressed to William James and his wife Alice; Rose reads the passage as "one of those double linguistic takes or backhanders in which [Alice James] revels (one of Freud's 'witty hysterics')" ("Jeffrey Masson and Alice James," 186).

14. See the diary entry in which Alice James notes approvingly William's use of the term "abandon" to designate the circumscription of the field of consciousness in the "nervous victim" or hysteric. Although by her own account Alice has "never unfortunately been able to abandon my consciousness and get five minutes' rest," she recalls having "passed through an infinite succession of conscious abandonments," in which,

> owing to some physical weakness, excess of nervous susceptibility, the moral power *pauses*, as it were for a moment, and refuses to maintain muscular sanity, worn out with the strain of its constabulary functions. As I used to sit immovable reading in the library with waves of violent inclination suddenly invading my muscles taking some one of their myriad forms such as throwing myself out of the window, or knocking off the head of the benignant pater as he sat with his silver locks, writing at his table, it used to seem to me that the only difference between me and the insane was that I had not only all the horrors and suffering of insanity but the duties of doctor, nurse, and strait-jacket imposed upon me, too. Conceive of never being without the sense that if you let yourself go for a moment your mechanism will fall into pie and that at some given moment you must abandon it all, let the dykes break and the flood sweep in, acknowledging yourself abjectly impotent before the immutable laws. (*Diary*, 149)

She has, in the wake of these recollected episodes, not only "to 'abandon' my brain, as it were," but, in the following entry, to "'abandon' the rhetorical part of me and forego the eloquent peroration with which I meant to embellish the above, on the ignorant asininity of the medical profession in its treatment of nervous disorders. The seething part of me has also given out and had to be abandoned." In a further allusion to William's essay, she refers to what remains after the succession of abandonments (and what will remain after death) as "the *residuum*" (*Diary*, 148–50). In textual terms, the *residuum* may be understood as what remains (of rhetoric) once a grammatical decoding or (of grammar) once a rhetorical analysis has taken place.

15. As noted in the preceding chapter, de Man makes this argument in "Autobiography as De-Facement," 77. Derrida observes that the voice given by means of the figure of prosopopoeia, while fictive, "already haunts any said real or present voice" ("Mnemosyne," 26).

16. See also the passage quoted by Yeazell: "In those ghastly days, when I was by myself in the little house in Mt. Vernon St., how I longed to flee in to the firemen next door & escape from the 'Alone! Alone!' that echoed thro' the house, rustled down the stairs, whispered from the walls & confronted me, like a material presence, as I sat waiting, counting the moments as they turned themselves from today into tomorrow" (*Death and Letters*, 24–25). As Yeazell notes, it is as such a "material presence" that Spencer Brydon's alter ego confronts him in Henry James's autobiographically based story, "The Jolly Corner." I have analyzed the pivotal role of prosopopoeia in James's late tale in "A Jamesian About-Face: Notes on 'The Jolly Corner.'" The "quasi-hallucinatory refrain which passes through the male line" of the James family (Rose, "Jeffrey Masson and Alice James," 189)—the notorious "vastation" of Henry Sr. (in which he hallucinates "some damned shape squatting invisible to me within the precincts of the room and raying out from his fetid personality influences fatal to life") and William's account in *The Varieties of Religious Experience* of a depressive episode (in which "a horrible fear of my own existence" coincides with "the image of an epileptic patient whom I had seen in the asylum," who "sat there like a sort of sculptured Egyptian cat or Peruvian mummy . . . looking absolutely non-human")—must also be read in this light (Rose, "Jeffrey Masson and Alice James," 189; Strouse, *Alice James*, 127, 129). If, as Rose suggests, hallucination (like telepathy) is to be understood as "the vanishing point of what was to become the psychoanalytic account of hysteria" (189), it is precisely at this point that

rhetorical reading can intervene to supplement that account. It is likewise in these (rhetorical) terms that the conjuring, reanimating power of the name—in particular, the name "William"—offers itself to be read in Alice James's journal. In the entry for July 16, 1889, Alice writes of "a curious psychological problem to solve, the spell cast over the French race by the commonplace name of William." She is responding to Jules Lemaître's commentary on an adaptation of Shakespeare, and she addresses him directly: "I should greatly like to know just what the sound *William* stands for in your mind and that of your kind" (*Diary*, 50). In the entry that follows, "William" materializes before her:

> I must try and pull myself together and record the somewhat devastating episode of July 18th when Harry after a much longer absence than usual presented himself, doubled by William!! We had just finished luncheon and were talking of something or other when H. suddenly said, with a queer look upon his face, 'I must tell you something!' 'You're not going to be married!' shrieked I. 'No, but William is here . . . and is waiting now in the Holly Walk for the news to be broken to you and if you *survive*, I'm to tie my handkerch[ief] to the balcony.' Enter Wm. *not* à la Romeo via the balcony; the prose of our century to say nothing of our consanguinity making it super[er]ogatory.

The other William—Shakespeare—is once again inscribed as William James is conjured by his sister's sounding of his name. "He doesn't look [much] older for the five years, and all that there is to be said of him, of course, is that he is simply himself." But the simplicity of this self-identity and its affirmation is belied by what follows in the journal passage, and Alice goes on to write of her brother as

> a creature who speaks in another language as H. says from the rest of mankind and who would lend life and charm to a treadmill. What a strange experience it was, to have *what has seemed so dead and gone* all these years suddenly bloom before one . . . redolent with the exquisite *family* perfume of the days gone by, made of the allusions, the memories and the point of view in common, so that my floating-particle sense was lost for an hour or so in the illusion that what is forever shattered had sprung up anew, and existed outside of our memories. . . . (*Diary*, 51–52, some emphasis added)

17. A citation of this passage from the diary closes the chapter of Strouse's biography entitled "Gains and Losses." In a letter to her sister-in-law dated February 5, 1890, Alice James urges her to instill in her children "the most conservative habits with regard to their family letters . . . they will have priceless value in time." She then recounts the arrival of the Davenport containing her parents' old letters: "I fell upon them and

wallowed for two days in the strangest & most vivid experience. I had to tear myself away for pathologic causes & do not dare return yet, but they are perpetually soliciting me; like living things sucking me back into the succulent past out of this anomalous death in life—an existence as juicy as that of a dried cod-fish!" (*Death and Letters*, 180).

18. I engage this figuration of the past in "Understanding Allegories: Reading *The Portrait of a Lady*."

19. Elsewhere in the diary, it is the "first-timeness" of events and passages that seems to Alice James to guarantee their "survival" in memory (*Diary*, 128).

20. Jacobus cites Strouse's assertion that, for Alice James, "the anomalous literary realm occupied by the diary lay safely within the feminine province of the personal" (Jacobus, *Reading Woman*, 251). One aim of the present reading is to suggest that the text of the journal is neither safe nor personal. In part, this is to argue that the diary is not simply a private document but is rather apostrophic, addressed to some other or others (Katharine Loring noted repeatedly that Alice James meant for her record to be published one day and wrote for publication). Indeed, in James's case public and private "inhabit exactly the same language, in the way that a postcard is at once public and private" (Hartman, Introduction, xxvi). But it is important to preserve the alternative possibility that the journal's language may be "[i]ntended for no one and nothing, [a] remainder of language" that "may well be language in its purity, nonreferentiality and virtuality" (Hamacher, "History, Teary," 71).

21. This is the irony operative, for example, in Henry James's "The Jolly Corner" and in *The Sense of the Past*.

22. Cf. Hamacher, "Journals, Politics" (a passage cited in Part I, above): "History, this vague abstraction, seems then and now to function as a powerful means of homogenizing and making a taboo out of history—namely, *that* history which exists only concretely, singularly, idiosyncratically, painfully" (463). Such is the history of Alice James.

Chapter 8

1. Jarman is quoted in Minty Clinch, "Positive Direction," 63.

2. The journals are also in part a tangle of citations from classical literature on horticulture. On Jarman's practice of "ambush by quotation" in *Modern Nature*, see Daniel O'Quinn, "Gardening, History and the Escape from Time."

3. "Slowly the garden acquired a new meaning—the plants struggling against biting winds and Death Valley sun merged with Derek's struggle with illness, then contrasted with it, as the flowers blossomed while Derek faded" (Collins, Preface, 5). Jarman himself glosses the allegorical character of his garden in the text of *Modern Nature*:

> . . . I [came here] after the discovery of my seropositivity. Behind the facade my life is at sixes and sevens. I water the roses and wonder whether I will see them bloom. I plant my herbal garden as a panacea, read up on all the aches and pains that plants will cure—and know they are not going to help. The garden as pharmacopoeia has failed.
>
> Yet there is a thrill in watching the plants spring up that gives me hope.
>
> Even so, I find myself unable to record the disaster that has befallen some of my friends, particularly dear Howard [Brookner], who I miss more than imagination. He wanders into my mind, as he wandered out of a stormy night 18 months ago. (179)

He extends the figural relation to landscape in general, writing, for example, of "Lovers shrivelled and parched like the landscape" (129) and reflects on the art of memory peculiar to the garden: "The dew of the garden was mixed in the morning with the sweet fragrance of his memories. The flowers are his mouth, the breeze his breath, the rose has been moistened by the dew of his cheeks. Therefore I love gardens madly, for at all times they make me remember him who I love" (129).

4. Elsewhere in *Modern Nature*, the wind's affective impact ranges from anxiety to depression to madness: "The wind blows—it unsettles me. The constant buffeting scatters thoughts and concentration" (85); "I feel as tangled as the sheets which move through the hurricane of my dreams" (157); "The wind blew terribly, it brings on depression. Didn't the Sirocco drive the unwary mad?" (287).

5. The diary entries in *Modern Nature* are punctuated by accounts of subsequent storms and their cost to the local landscape:

> The storm has taken its toll at Dungeness. The telephone pole outside my window has snapped and swings back and forth in the wind supported only by the wires. The new greenhouse has been stripped of its glass, and the garage that took such a battering in the hurricane has collapsed and is being burnt at the side of the road. The army base measured gusts of 120 mph.
>
> My garden was flattened. At least half of the driftwood poles were down and one of the metal buoys had entirely vanished. The house itself was undamaged. . . . But the greatest loss is among the plants, which have been burnt by the salt wind and look very sad. (227–28)

> A wild wind roared through the night, chasing sleep to the edge of dawn. With the tide the storm came at midnight. . . . My heart missed a beat at each violent gust. On our way here we saw a Mini that had come off the road and sunk to its roof in a drainage ditch. Branches off trees, fallen chimney pots and slates marked the passing of the last Great Storm two weeks ago.
>
> Crystalline sunlight, all the dark humours blown away by the wind. . . . Spring comes despite the scorching gales which boil the leaves of daffodils like spinach. Today the sun shines on and on to make amends. (235)

> The garden feels under siege this winter. In my absence the gales have freeze-dried everything. (250)

6. O'Quinn notes the figurative import of these observations: "[W]e find Jarman describing in some detail how high winds have already defoliated his rosemary plants and are presently destroying his newly flowering daffodils. It is not insignificant that previous entries identify rosemary as 'the herb sacred to remembrance, and therefore to friendship' and suggest that daffodils first came to Britain in the packs of Roman soldiers because their bulbs were used by Galen to 'glue together wounds and gashes.' The figurative destruction of memory *and* the potential for healing in Jarman's description of his ravaged garden is interrupted by a memory of being in another garden in ruin, as Jarman turns to a reminiscence of the Borghese Gardens shortly after the Second World War" ("Gardening, History" ms., 5).

7. Horkheimer's experiment is recounted in Werner Hamacher, "Journals, Politics," 457.

8. Cf. Jarman's *The Last of England*: "I don't believe in the gold at the end of the rainbow, but I do believe in the rainbow" (212). Writing of the false promise of film, Jarman cites Vincent Canby's scathing review of *War Requiem* and remarks: "Since most of the cinema is an enormous irrelevance, a medium that has crossed the boundaries of intelligence in a very few hands, it does not worry me. No-one except fools expected to find much at the end of this rainbow" (*Modern Nature*, 234).

9. Cf. the *Oxford English Dictionary*'s definition of "yellow" as descriptive of journalism: "Applied to newspapers (or writers of newspaper articles) of a recklessly or unscrupulously sensational character. A use derived from the appearance in 1895 of a number of the *New York World* in which a child in a yellow dress ('The Yellow Kid') was the central figure of the cartoon, this being an experiment in colour-printing designed to attract purchasers."

10. A number of the paintings were included in the Barbican Art

Gallery's 1996 retrospective of Jarman's work, documented in a catalogue entitled *Derek Jarman: A Portrait.*

11. The headline's reference is to Jarman's role as producer of the Pet Shop Boys' world tour. The yellow press plagues him even in his dreams: "Dreamt that ——— sodomized ——— in a new Greenaway film, with the critic of the *Guardian* writing columns of praise that were published in the *Sun*" (*Modern Nature*, 167).

12. In "Biodegradables," Derrida advances

> the following *nontheorem* on the subject of the figurative "biodegradability" of what are commonly called texts, or at least . . . of publications. One cannot wager publicly on the survival of an archive without thereby giving it an extra chance. As if the wager on the survival itself contributed to the survival. Thus, the wager cannot take the form of a *theoretical* hypothesis on the subject of what will happen objectively in an autonomous field. That is why I spoke of a *nontheorem*. Like any discourse on the wager, a wager intervenes performatively in the field and partially determines it. It feigns "objective" and theoretical speculation while in fact it performs a practical transformation of its object. . . . By definition, and this is why there is wagering and performative intervention of the wager, no calculation will ever be able to master the "biodegradability" to come of a document. (836)

13. Jarman recounts, for example, the tale of the wind god's revenge:

> The bluebell, *Hyacinthus nonscriptus*, is the hyacinth of the ancients, the flower of grief and mourning. Hyacinth, son of the king of Sparta, whose sparkling blue eyes and jet black hair enflamed Phoebus Apollo, whipped Zephyrus into a frenzy of desire; but the boy loved the sun god best, causing the wild west wind to seek a terrible revenge. One day as Hyacinth and Apollo were playing quoits Zephyrus caught a quoit in a whirlwind and smashed the boy's beautiful face, killing him. Grief-stricken, Apollo raised the purple flower from the drops of blood on which he traced the letters *ai ai*, so his anguish would forever echo through the spring.
>
> Whenever you walk in a sunny bluebell wood, remember it is the heart of a passionate love. It is dangerous to kiss there, as the wind sighing in the branches will want to blow you and the boy apart. Your love may wilt and die as quickly as the flowers you pick, your hands will be stained with blood.
>
> So leave the wood in peace, empty-handed. For the blue-eyed flower with its heavy fragrance only belongs to the sun.
>
> And remember that Ovid said that Sparta was not ashamed of having produced Hyacinth, *for he is honored there to this very day, and every year the Hyacinthian games are celebrated with festive displays, in accordance with ancient usage.* (*Modern Nature*, 61–62)

In this context, Jarman cannot resist an editorial gloss: "We learned nothing of the love myth of these heroes in the 1950's—Ovid was off-limits. Instead we marched to the beat of Caesar's interminable *Gallic Wars*. . . . War underpinned an English education" (*Modern Nature*, 63).

In another instance, Jarman describes the procession sponsored by the French government to mark the 200th anniversary of the Bastille storming, invoking still other gods: "before this—the climactic moment—the sound on my TV faded in an eerie wind, the sort you get in horror movies. After it had blown through the proceedings for several minutes the commentator informed us that this was the official soundtrack. I can't have been the only one who had thought the gods were blowing cold on so much wind" (110).

14. The film, whose title never appears in the journal, is Ivens's *Die Windrose* (1955–56).

Works Cited

Althusser, Louis. "Ideology and Ideological State Apparatuses." In *Lenin and Philosophy*. Translated by Ben Brewster. New York: Monthly Review Press, 127–86.

Balfour, Ian. "'Difficult Reading': De Man's Itineraries." In Hamacher, Hertz, and Keenan, eds., *Responses*, 6–20.

Barbican Art Gallery. *Derek Jarman: A Portrait* [catalog of a retrospective showing of Jarman's paintings]. London: Thames and Hudson, 1996.

Bate, Walter Jackson. "The Crisis in English Studies." *Harvard Magazine* 85, no. 1 (September–October 1982): 46–53.

Bazin, André. *What is Cinema?* Translated by Hugh Gray. Berkeley: University of California Press, 1967.

Benjamin, Walter. *Illuminations*. Edited by Hannah Arendt. New York: Schocken Books, 1968.

———. Letter to Martin Buber, February 23, 1927. In "Moscow Diary," 132–33.

———. "Moscow Diary." *October* 35 (winter 1985): 9–124.

———. "Theses on the Concept of History." In *Illuminations*, 253–64.

Bloom, Allan. *The Closing of the American Mind*. New York: Simon and Schuster, 1987.

Brenkman, John. "Fascist Commitments." In Hamacher, Hertz, and Keenan, eds., *Responses*, 21–35.

Butler, Jeremy. "Notes on the Soap Opera Apparatus: Televisual Style and *As the World Turns*." *Cinema Journal* 25, no. 3 (spring 1986).

Cavell, Stanley. "The Fact of Television." In *Themes Out of School: Effects and Causes*, 235–68. San Francisco: North Point Press, 1984.

———. *The World Viewed.* Cambridge, Mass.: Harvard University Press, 1979.

Charlesworth, Sarah. *Unwriting: Notes on Modern History* [catalog of art show]. Edinburgh: New 57 Gallery, 1979.

Chase, Cynthia. "Trappings of an Education." In Hamacher, Hertz, and Keenan, eds., *Responses,* 44–79.

Clark, Ramsay. "A War Crime." *The Nation,* March 11, 1991, 308–9.

Clinch, Minty. "Positive Direction." *The Observer Magazine,* October 13, 1991, 63.

CNN [Cable News Network]. Transcripts of televised news broadcasts, September 3, 1996.

Collins, Keith. Preface to *Derek Jarman's Garden,* by Derek Jarman. London: Thames and Hudson, 1995.

Creech, James, Peggy Kamuf, and Jane Todd. "Deconstruction in America: An Interview with Jacques Derrida." *Society for Critical Exchange* 17 (winter 1985): 1–55.

de Graef, Ortwin. "Aspects of the Context of Paul de Man's Earliest Publications." In Hamacher, Hertz, and Keenan, eds., *Responses,* 96–115.

de Man, Paul. "Aesthetic Formalization: Kleist's *Über das Marionettentheater.*" In *Rhetoric of Romanticism,* 263–90.

———. *Aesthetic Ideology.* Edited by Andrzej Warminski. Minneapolis: University of Minnesota Press, 1996.

———. *Allegories of Reading: Figural Language in Rousseau, Nietzsche, Rilke and Proust.* New Haven, Conn.: Yale University Press, 1979.

———. "Allegory (*Julie*)." In *Allegories of Reading,* 188–220.

———. "Anthropomorphism and Trope in the Lyric." In *Rhetoric of Romanticism,* 239–62.

———. "Autobiography as De-facement." In *Rhetoric of Romanticism,*" 67–81.

———. *Blindness and Insight: Essays in the Rhetoric of Contemporary Criticism.* 2d rev. ed. Minneapolis: University of Minnesota Press, 1983.

———. "Criticism and Crisis." In *Blindness and Insight,* 3–19.

———. "Criticism and Literary History." In *Wartime Journalism,* 313–14.

———. "Culture and Art. Art as Mirror of the Essence of Nations: Considerations on 'Geist der Nationen' by A. E. Brinckmann." In *Wartime Journalism,* 302–3.

———. "Le destin de la Flandre." In *Wartime Journalism,* 139–40.

———. "Dialogue and Dialogism." In *Resistance to Theory,* 106–14.

———. "Hypogram and Inscription." In *Resistance to Theory,* 27–53.

———. "Interview with Stephano Rosso." In *Resistance to Theory*, 115–21.
———. "Introduction à la littérature allemande contemporaine." In *Wartime Journalism*, 200–1.
———. "Journal de la France (Tome II) par Alfred Fabre-Luce." In *Wartime Journalism*, 253–54.
———. "Les Juifs dans la littérature actuelle." In *Wartime Journalism*, 45.
———. "Kant and Schiller." In *Aesthetic Ideology*, 129–62.
———. "Kant's Materialism." In *Aesthetic Ideology*, 119–28.
———. "Metaphor (*Second Discourse*)." In *Allegories of Reading*, 135–59.
———. "Notre chronique littéraire: Charles Péguy." In *Wartime Journalism*, 85–86.
———. "People and Books. A View on Contemporary German Literature." In *Wartime Journalism*, 325–26.
———. "Phenomenality and Materiality in Kant." In *Aesthetic Ideology*, 70–90.
———. Preface to *Allegories of Reading*, ix–xi.
———. "Le problème de l'adolescence." In *Wartime Journalism*, 246–47.
———. "Promises (*Social Contract*)." In *Allegories of Reading*, 246–77.
———. "A la recherche d'un nouveau mode d'expression." In *Wartime Journalism*, 208–9.
———. *The Resistance to Theory*. Minneapolis: University of Minnesota Press, 1986.
———. "The Resistance to Theory." In *Resistance to Theory*, 3–20.
———. "The Return to Philology." In *Resistance to Theory*, 21–26.
———. "The Rhetoric of Blindness: Jacques Derrida's Reading of Rousseau." In *Blindness and Insight*, 102–41.
———. *The Rhetoric of Romanticism*. New York: Columbia University Press, 1984.
———. "The Rhetoric of Temporality." In *Blindness and Insight*, 187–228.
———. "Semiology and Rhetoric." In *Allegories of Reading*, 3–19.
———. "Shelley Disfigured." In *Rhetoric of Romanticism*, 93–123.
———. "Universalisme de Goethe. 'Les Affinités Electives' (1)." In *Wartime Journalism*, 238–39.
———. "*Voir la figure*, de Jacques Chardonne (1)." In *Wartime Journalism*, 158–59.
———. *Wartime Journalism, 1939–1943*. Edited by Werner Hamacher, Neil Hertz, and Thomas Keenan. Lincoln: University of Nebraska Press, 1988.

Derrida, Jacques. "The Art of Memoires." In *Memoires*, 45–88.
———. "Biodegradables: Seven Diary Fragments." Translated by Peggy Kamuf. *Critical Inquiry* 15, no. 4 (summer 1989): 812–73.
———. *De l'esprit. Heidegger et la question.* Paris: Galilee, 1987.
———. "In Discussion with Christopher Norris." In *Deconstruction II.* New York: St. Martin's Press, 1989.
———. "The Laws of Reflection: Nelson Mandela, in Admiration." In *For Nelson Mandela.* Edited by Jacques Derrida and Mustapha Tlili. New York: Henry Holt, 1987.
———. "Letter to a Japanese Friend." In *Derrida and Différance*, edited by David Wood and Robert Bernasconi, 107–27. Coventry: Parousia Press, 1985.
———. "Like the Sound of the Sea Deep Within a Shell: Paul de Man's War." Translated by Peggy Kamuf. In Hamacher, Hertz, and Keenan, eds., *Responses*, 127–64.
———. *Margins of Philosophy.* Translated by Alan Bass. Chicago: University of Chicago Press, 1982.
———. *Memoires: For Paul de Man.* Translated by Cecile Lindsay, Jonathan Culler, and Eduardo Cadava. New York: Columbia University Press, 1986.
———. "Mnemosyne." In *Memoires*, 1–43.
———. "Mochlos; or, The Conflict of the Faculties." In *Logomachia: The Conflict of the Faculties*, edited by Richard Rand, 1–34. Lincoln: University of Nebraska Press, 1992.
———. *Of Grammatology.* Translated by Gayatri Chakravorty Spivak. Baltimore, Md.: Johns Hopkins University Press, 1975.
———. *Positions.* Translated by Alan Bass. Chicago: University of Chicago Press, 1982.
———. "The Principle of Reason: The University in the Eyes of its Pupils." Translated by Catherine Porter and Edward P. Morris. *diacritics* 13, no. 3 (fall 1983): 3–20.
———. "Signature Event Context." In *Margins of Philosophy*, 307–30.
———. "Some Statements and Truisms about Neo-logisms, Newisms, Postisms, Parasitisms, and Other Small Seismisms." In *The States of "Theory"*, edited by David Carroll. New York: Columbia University Press, 1990.
Dienst, Richard. *Still Life in Real Time: Theory After Television.* Durham, N.C.: Duke University Press, 1994.
Doane, Mary Ann. "Information, Crisis, Catastrophe." In *Logics of Tele-*

vision: Essays in Cultural Criticism, edited by Patricia Mellencamp, 222–39. Bloomington: University of Indiana Press, 1990.

Edel, Leon. "Introduction: A Portrait of Alice James." In A. James, *Diary of Alice James*, 1–22.

———. Preface to *Diary of Alice James*, vii–xiii.

Esch, Deborah. "A Jamesian About-Face: Notes on 'The Jolly Corner.'" *English Literary History* 50, no. 3 (fall 1983): 587–605.

———. "Promissory Notes: The Prescription of the Future in *The Princess Casamassima*." *American Literary History* 1, no. 2 (summer 1989): 484–500.

———. "Understanding Allegories: Reading *The Portrait of a Lady*." In *Modern Critical Interpretations: The Portrait of a Lady*, edited by Harold Bloom, 131–53. New Haven, Conn.: Chelsea House, 1987.

Feuer, Jane. "The Concept of Live Television: Ontology as Ideology." In *Television: Critical Approaches*, edited by E. Ann Kaplan, 12–22. Frederick, Md.: University Publications of America, 1982.

Findlay, Len. "Otherwise Engaged: Postmodernism and the Resistance to History." *English Studies in Canada* 14, no. 4 (December 1988): 383–99.

Flitterman-Lewis, Sandy. "All's Well that Doesn't End: Soap Opera and the Marriage Motif." *camera obscura* 16 (January 1988): 119–27.

Fraser, Graham. "U.S. Launches Second Attack on Iraq." *Globe and Mail*, September 4, 1996, A1.

Friedman, Thomas L. "Desert Fog." *New York Times*, February 24, 1991, 4:1.

Gallagher, Catherine. "Blindness and Hindsight." In Hamacher, Hertz, and Keenan, eds., *Responses*, 204–7.

Gasché, Rodolphe. "Edges of Understanding." In Hamacher, Hertz, and Keenan, eds., *Responses*, 208–20.

———. Introduction to Warminski, *Readings in Interpretation*, ix–xxvi.

Godzich, Wlad. "The Culture of Illiteracy." *Enclitic* 15/16 (1984): 27–35.

———. "Religion, the State, and Post(al) Modernism." Afterword to Weber, *Institution and Interpretation*, 153–64.

———. "The Tiger on the Paper Mat." Foreword to de Man, *Resistance to Theory*, ix–xviii.

Goethe, Johann Wolfgang von. *Die Wahlverwandtschaften*. Frankfurt am Main: Insel, 1976. *The Elective Affinities*. Translated by James A. Froude and R. Dillon Boylan. New York: Frederick Ungar, 1962.

Grachos, Louis. "Contemporary Currents: Sarah Charlesworth" [catalog of art show]. New York: The Queens Museum of Art, 1992.

Graff, Gerald. "Looking Past the de Man Case." In Hamacher, Hertz, and Keenan, eds., *Responses*, 246–54.
Greenaway, Peter. *The Draughtsman's Contract* [published script of film]. London: British Film Institute, 1982.
Greenblatt, Stephen, and Giles Gunn, eds. *Redrawing the Boundaries: The Transformation of English and American Literary Studies*. New York: Modern Language Association, 1992.
"Gulf War Kills Dhaka Boy." *Globe and Mail*, February 24, 1991, A11.
Hamacher, Werner. "History, Teary." *Yale French Studies* 74 (1988): 67–94.
———. "Journals, Politics." Translated by Peter Burgard et al. In Hamacher, Hertz, and Keenan, eds., *Responses*, 438–65.
Hamacher, Werner, Neil Hertz, and Thomas Keenan. "Paul de Man: A Chronology, 1919–1949." In Hamacher, Hertz, and Keenan, eds., *Responses*, xi–xxi.
———, eds. *Responses: On Paul de Man's Wartime Journalism*. Lincoln: University of Nebraska Press, 1989.
Hartman, Geoffrey. "History and Judgment: The Case of Paul de Man." *History and Memory* (1989).
———. "Looking Back on Paul de Man." In Waters and Godzich, eds., *Reading de Man Reading*, 3–24.
———. *Saving the Text*. Baltimore, Md.: Johns Hopkins University Press, 1981.
Heath, Stephen, and Gillian Skirrow. "Television: A World in Action." *Screen* 18, no. 2 (summer 1977).
Higgins, Lynne A. Review of de Man, *Wartime Journalism, 1939–1943*, and Hamacher, Hertz, and Keenan, eds., *Responses*. *South Central Review* 6, no. 2 (summer 1989).
"Iraqis Surrender to Italian TV." *New York Times*, February 23, 1991, A6.
Jacobs, David. Introduction to Van Wormer, *Knots Landing*.
Jacobus, Mary. *Reading Woman: Essays in Feminist Criticism*. New York: Columbia University Press, 1986.
James, Alice. *The Death and Letters of Alice James*. Edited by Ruth Bernard Yeazell. Berkeley: University of California Press, 1981.
———. *The Diary of Alice James*. Edited by Leon Edel. Harmondsworth: Penguin, 1964.
James, Henry. *The Art of the Novel*. Edited by R. P. Blackmur. New York: Scribner's, 1962.

———. Preface to *What Maisie Knew*, 5–13. Harmondsworth: Penguin, 1984.

James, William. "The Hidden Self." In *A William James Reader*, edited by Gay Wilson Allen. Boston: Houghton Mifflin Co., 1971.

———. *The Varieties of Religious Experience*. New York: Modern Library, 1929.

Jameson, Fredric. *Marxism and Form*. Princeton, N.J.: Princeton University Press, 1971.

———. *Postmodernism; or, the Cultural Logic of Late Capitalism*. Durham, N.C.: Duke University Press, 1991.

Jarman, Derek. *At Your Own Risk: A Saint's Testament*. Woodstock, N.Y.: Overlook Press, 1993.

———. *Chroma*. London: Vintage, 1995.

———. *The Last of England*. London: Constable, 1987.

———. *Modern Nature*. London: Vintage, 1991.

———. *Queer* [painting exhibit]. Potsdam: Filmmuseum Potsdam, 1993.

[Jarman, Derek.] Obituary of Derek Jarman. *Times* (London), February 21, 1994, 17.

Johnson, Barbara. "Preface to the Paperback Edition: A Note on the Wartime Writings of Paul de Man." In *A World of Difference*. 2d ed. Baltimore, Md.: Johns Hopkins University Press, 1988.

Kamuf, Peggy. "Impositions: A Violent Dawn at *Le Soir*." In Hamacher, Hertz, and Keenan, eds., *Responses*, 255–65.

———. "Pieces of Resistance." In Waters and Godzich, eds., *Reading de Man Reading*, 136–54.

Kaplan, Alice Yaeger. "Paul de Man, *Le Soir*, and the Francophone Collaboration (1940–1942)." In Hamacher, Hertz, and Keenan, eds., *Responses*, 266–84.

Keenan, Thomas. "Have You Seen Your World Today?" *Art Journal* (winter 1995): 102–5.

Kernan, Alvin. *The Death of Literature*. New Haven, Conn.: Yale University Press, 1990.

———. "The Death of Literature." *Princeton Alumni Weekly* 92, no. 8 (January 22, 1992): 11–15.

Klein, Richard. "The Blindness of Hyperboles; the Ellipses of Insight." *diacritics* 3, no. 2 (1973).

Knots Landing. CBS television broadcast.

Lacoue-Labarthe, Philippe. *La fiction du politique*. Paris: Christian Bourgois, 1987.
Lapham, Lewis H. "Economic Correctness." *Harper's*, no. 1761 (February 1997).
Lardner, James. "War of the Words." *Washington Post*, March 6, 1983, G1, G10.
Lewes, George Henry. *Life and Works of Goethe*. London: J. M. Dent, 1908.
Lewis, Mark, and Andrew Payne. "The Ghost Dance: An Interview with Jacques Derrida." *Public* 2 (1989): 60–66.
Littwin, Susan. "Flying Without a Net on *Knots*." *TV Guide* 569 (November 28, 1987): 6.
Longinus. *On the Sublime*. Cambridge, Mass.: Harvard University Press, 1973.
Lorch, Donatella. "For a Jubilant Crowd in Kuwait City, It's Victory Signs, Tears and Kisses." *New York Times*, February 23, 1991, A6.
Lyotard, Jean-François. "Brief Reflections on Popular Culture." *ICA Documents* 4 [special issue on "Postmodernism"] (1986): 58.
Miller, J. Hillis. "A Buchstäbliches Reading of *The Elective Affinities*." *Glyph* 6 (1979): 1–23.
Noguchi, Isamu. *The Isamu Noguchi Garden Museum*. New York: Harry N. Abrams, 1987.
O'Quinn, Daniel. "Gardening, History and the Escape from Time: Derek Jarman's *Modern Nature*." *October* 89 (Summer 1999).
Ottaway, David B. "U.S. Alerted to Embassy Bugs in '79." *Washington Post*, April 23, 1987, A1, A17.
Penley, Constance, and Andrew Ross. "Couch Potatoes Aren't Dupes." *New York Times*, March 11, 1991.
Prinn, Jonathan. "Gay Age of Consent Vote in the Balance." *Times* (London), February 21, 1994, 1.
Proust, Marcel. *Remembrance of Things Past*. Translated by C. K. Scott Moncrieff and Terence Kilmartin. New York: Random House, 1981.
Rose, Jacqueline. "Jeffrey Masson and Alice James." *Oxford Literary Review* 8, no. 1–2 [special issue on "Sexual Difference"] (1986): 185–92.
Rosenberg, Howard. "High Noon in Television's High Court." *Los Angeles Times*, October 14, 1991, F10.
"Saddam Smashes CIA Bid to Topple Him." *Toronto Star*, September 8, 1996, A12.
Sartre, Jean-Paul. "Qu'est-ce qu'un collaborateur?" In *Situations III*, 43–61. Paris: Gallimard, 1949.

Schmitt, Eric. "Racing Through the Darkness in Pursuit of Scuds." *New York Times*, February 24, 1991, A9.
Sciolino, Elaine. "Staying Power: How Saddam Hussein Survives by Losing." *New York Times*, September 8, 1996, 4:1.
"Security at the American Embassy in Moscow and the United States–Soviet Embassy Exchange Agreements." *Hearings Before the Subcommittee on International Operations of the Committee on Foreign Affairs, House of Representatives*, April 22, 1987, 35–127. Washington: U.S. Government Printing Office, 1988.
Spivak, Gayatri Chakravorty. *In Other Worlds: Essays in Cultural Politics*. New York: Methuen, 1987.
———. Translator's preface to *Of Grammatology*, by Jacques Derrida, lx–lxxxvii.
Strouse, Jean. *Alice James: A Biography*. Boston: Houghton Mifflin Co., 1980.
Taubin, Amy. "No News is Good News." *Village Voice*, September 5, 1989, 55.
Van Wormer, Laura. *Knots Landing: The Saga of Seaview Circle*. New York: Doubleday, 1986.
Virilio, Paul. *L'écran du desert: Chroniques de guerre*. Paris: Galilee, 1991.
"Voting for Change." *Times* (London), February 21, 1994, 15.
Warminski, Andrzej. "Deconstruction in America/Heidegger Reading Hölderlin." *Critical Exchange* 17 (winter 1985): 45–59.
———. "Epigraphs" and "Terrible Reading." In Hamacher, Hertz, and Keenan, eds., *Responses*, 386–96.
———. "Reading Over Endless Histories: Henry James's *Altar of the Dead*." *Yale French Studies* 74 (1988): 261–84.
———. *Readings in Interpretation: Hölderlin, Hegel, Heidegger*. Minneapolis: University of Minnesota Press, 1987.
Waters, Lindsay, and Wlad Godzich, eds. *Reading de Man Reading*. Minneapolis: University of Minnesota Press, 1989.
Watney, Simon. "Derek Jarman." *Artforum* (May 1994): 84–85, 119, 125.
Weber, Samuel. *Institution and Interpretation*. Minneapolis: University of Minnesota Press.
———. Introduction to *Demarcating the Disciplines*, edited by Samuel Weber, ix–xii. Glyph Textual Studies, vol. 1. Minneapolis: University of Minnesota Press, 1986.
———. *Mass Mediauras*. Stanford, Calif.: Stanford University Press, 1996.

———. "The Media and the War." *Alphabet City* 1, no. 1 (summer 1991): 22–26.

———. "The Monument Disfigured." In Hamacher, Hertz, and Keenan, eds., *Responses*, 404–25.

Wellek, René. "Destroying Literary Studies." *The New Criterion* 2, no. 4 (December 1983): 1–8.

"When Will It Be?", *Globe and Mail*, January 20, 1996, D6.

Williams, Scott. "Reliance on TV Peaks with Gulf War." *Globe and Mail*, May 2, 1991, C5.

Woodward, Kenneth L., et al. "A New Look At Lit Crit." *Newsweek*, June 22, 1981, 80–83.

Wyver, John. "Television and Postmodernism." *ICA Documents* 4 [special issue on "Postmodernism"] (1986): 52–54.

Yeazell, Ruth Bernard, ed. Introduction to *Death and Letters of Alice James*, 1–45. Berkeley: University of California Press, 1981.

Žižek, Slavoj. *The Sublime Object of Ideology*. London: Verso, 1989.

Index

In this index an "f" after a number indicates a separate reference on the next page, and an "ff" indicates separate references on the next two pages. A continuous discussion over two or more pages is indicated by a span of page numbers, e.g., "57–59." *Passim* is used for a cluster of references in close but not consecutive sequence.

MERIDIAN

Crossing Aesthetics

Deborah Esch, *In the Event: Reading Journalism, Reading Theory*

Giorgio Agamben, *Potentialities: Collected Essays in Philosophy*

Jacques Derrida, *Adieu to Emmanuel Levinas*

E. S. Burt, *Poetry's Appeal: Nineteenth-Century French Lyric and the Political Space*

Werner Hamacher, *Premises: Essays on Philosophy and Literature from Kant to Celan*

Aris Fioretos, *The Gray Book*

Winfried Menninghaus, *In Praise of Nonsense: Kant and Bluebeard*

Giorgio Agamben, *The Man Without Content*

Giorgio Agamben, *The End of the Poem: Essays in Poetics*

Theodor W. Adorno, *Sound Figures*

Louis Marin, *Sublime Poussin*

Philippe Lacoue-Labarthe, *Poetry as Experience*

Jacques Derrida, *Resistances of Psychoanalysis*

Ernst Bloch, *Literary Essays*

Marc Froment-Meurice, *That Is to Say: Heidegger's Poetics*

Francis Ponge, *Soap*

Phillipe Lacoue-Labarthe, *Typography: Mimesis, Philosophy, Politics*

Giorgio Agamben, *Homo Sacer: Sovereign Power and Bare Life*

Emmanuel Levinas, *Of God Who Comes to Mind*

Bernard Stiegler, *Technics and Time, 1: The Fault of Epimetheus*

Werner Hamacher, *pleroma—Reading in Hegel*

Serge Leclaire, *Psychoanalyzing*

Serge Leclaire, *A Child Is Being Killed*

Sigmund Freud, *Writings on Art and Literature*

Cornelius Castoriadis, *World in Fragments: Writings on Politics, Society, Psychoanalysis, and the Imagination*

Thomas Keenan, *Fables of Responsibility: Aberrations and Predicaments in Ethics and Politics*

Emmanuel Levinas, *Proper Names*

Alexander García Düttmann, *At Odds with AIDS: Thinking and Talking About a Virus*

Maurice Blanchot, *Friendship*

Jean-Luc Nancy, *The Muses*

Massimo Cacciari, *Posthumous People: Vienna at the Turning Point*

David E. Wellbery, *The Specular Moment: Goethe's Early Lyric and the Beginnings of Romanticism*

Edmond Jabès, *The Little Book of Unsuspected Subversion*

Hans-Jost Frey, *Studies in Poetic Discourse: Mallarmé, Baudelaire, Rimbaud, Hölderlin*

Pierre Bourdieu, *The Rules of Art: Genesis and Structure of the Literary Field*

Nicolas Abraham, *Rhythms: On the Work, Translation, and Psychoanalysis*

Jacques Derrida, *On the Name*

David Wills, *Prosthesis*

Maurice Blanchot, *The Work of Fire*

Jacques Derrida, *Points ... : Interviews, 1974–1994*

J. Hillis Miller, *Topographies*

Philippe Lacoue-Labarthe, *Musica Ficta (Figures of Wagner)*

Jacques Derrida, *Aporias*

Emmanuel Levinas, *Outside the Subject*

Jean-François Lyotard, *Lessons on the Analytic Sublime*

Peter Fenves, *"Chatter": Language and History in Kierkegaard*

Jean-Luc Nancy, *The Experience of Freedom*

Jean-Joseph Goux, *Oedipus, Philosopher*

Haun Saussy, *The Problem of a Chinese Aesthetic*

Jean-Luc Nancy, *The Birth to Presence*

Library of Congress Cataloging-in-Publication Data

Esch, Deborah
In the event : reading journalism, reading theory / Deborah Esch.
p. cm. — (Meridian, crossing aesthetics)
Includes bibliographical references (p.) and index.
ISBN 0-8047-3250-7 (alk. paper). — ISBN 0-8047-3251-5
(pbk. : alk paper)
1. Journalism. I. Title. II. Series: Meridian (Stanford, Calif.)
PN4731.E66 1999
070.4—dc21 99-27628

This book is printed on acid-free, archival quality paper.

Original printing 1999
Last figure below indicates the year of this printing:
08 07 06 05 04 03 02 01 00 99

Typeset by James P. Brommer in 10.9/13 Garamond
and Lithos display